English G

Band B1

für das 5. Schuljahr
an Realschulen

English G
Band B1

Im Auftrage des Verlages herausgegeben und erarbeitet von
Prof. Hellmut Schwarz, Mannheim · Carl Taylor M.A., München · Prof. Franz Vettel, Heppenheim

in Zusammenarbeit mit der Fremdsprachenredaktion
Michael R. Ferguson M.A. (Projektleitung), Cedric J. Sherratt B.A., Susanne Döpper, Hartmut Tschepe; Martin Rosenthal

unter Mitarbeit von
Prof. Dr. Günter Nold, Frankfurt am Main/PH Ludwigsburg
sowie RL Edgar Niemeier, Oldenburg · RL Heinrich Baumgarten, Hitzacker

Beratende Mitwirkung
Schulamtsdirektor Edgar Dietz, Weil am Rhein · John Eastwood M.A., Street, Somerset ·
StD Udo J. Hennig, Neuwied · Prof. Dr. Liesel Hermes, Karlsruhe · RL Heinrich Krömer, Lathen ·
RR Eberhard Lange, Bramsche · MR Burkhart Nather, Mülheim (Ruhr) ·
RL Antje Traude, Heiligenhaus

Grafik
Robert Broomfield, Tunbridge Wells
sowie Roy Schofield, Cheam, und Gabriele Heinisch, Berlin

Layout
Peter Richter und Bernd Lenzner

Bild- und Liedquellen
s. Verzeichnis auf S. 128

Zusatzmaterialien zum vorliegenden Schülerbuch:
Workbook mit Einführungskurs (Best.-Nr. 51633), ohne Einführungskurs (51625)
Grammatikheft (50726) · Cassette zum Einführungskurs (40631)
Cassette zum Schülerbuch (51684)
Lernsoftware: English Coach Vokabeltrainer · English Coach Grammatiktrainer
Auf weitere Bestandteile des Lehrwerks *English G* wird im Lehrerhandbuch (51641) verwiesen.

---

1. Auflage ✔
Druck 13 12 11 10   Jahr 2000 99 98 97

Alle Drucke dieser Auflage können im
Unterricht nebeneinander verwendet werden.

© 1985 Cornelsen Verlag, Berlin
Das Werk und seine Teile sind urheberrechtlich
geschützt. Jede Verwertung in anderen als den
gesetzlich zugelassenen Fällen bedarf deshalb
der vorherigen schriftlichen Einwilligung
des Verlages.

Satz Adolph Fürst & Sohn, Berlin
Reproduktion Rembert Faeßer, Berlin
Druck Cornelsen Druck, Berlin
Bindearbeiten Fritzsche-Ludwig, Berlin

ISBN 3-464-05161-7 — broschiert
      3-464-05082-3 — gebunden

Bestellnummer 51617 — broschiert
              50823 — gebunden

 gedruckt auf säurefreiem Papier, umweltschonend hergestellt aus chlorfrei gebleichten Faserstoffen

Contents

Unit	Page	Parts of the unit	Main speech functions	Structures
	5	**Intro**duction: Four young people from Hatfield		
	7	Song: One, two, three, four		
1	8	**A**cquisition: A new boy at Park School	Auskunft über sich und andere geben; Begrüßung und Verabschiedung	Personal pronouns and the verb *be* in positive sentences, negative sentences, questions and short answers · Short forms and long forms: *I'm – I am* · Gender of nouns: *the boy → he, the girl → she, the name/school/rabbit → it* · Plural of nouns: *one boy – two boys*
	11 ○	Song: They're in my class at school		
	12	Text: **Oh!**		
	13	**Ex**ercises		
	15	**S**ummary		
2	17	Acquisition: Friends and families	Über die Familie sprechen; sagen, was jemand besitzt; sich und andere vorstellen	*have got* in positive sentences, negative sentences, questions and short answers · Short forms and long forms: *I've got – I have got* · Possessive form of nouns: *Dave's sister* · Possessive adjectives · Cardinal numbers 1-1000
	20	Text: **My family**		
	21	Exercises		
	25	Summary		
3	26	Acquisition: Activities in the home; going to the swimming-pool	Jemandem sagen, was er tun soll; sagen, was jemand gerade tut; zustimmen und ablehnen	Infinitive: *(to) be, (to) ask* · Imperative: *Help Tina, please.* · Present progressive in positive sentences, negative sentences, questions and short answers
	29 ○	Song: Brother John		
	30	Text: **No problem for Dave?**		
	31	Exercises		
	35	Summary		
4	36	Acquisition: Pets; Peanut the dog	Beschreiben, was vorhanden ist; sagen, was jemand tun muss; sagen, was jemand kann; um Erlaubnis bitten	*There is …/There are …* · Plural of nouns: *girl – girls, book – books, class – classes, family – families* · Irregular plurals: e.g. *man – men, woman – women* · Modal auxiliaries: *can, may, must*
	39 ○	Song: My friend Jack		
	40	Text: **A wet afternoon**		
	41	Exercises		
	45 ○	Extra Reading: **What are your favourite pets?**		
	46	Summary		
	47	**The calendar:** Months and seasons	Das Datum angeben	Ordinal numbers 1st-31st
5	48	Acquisition: Birthdays; Woodside, a village near Hatfield	Über Geburtstage sprechen; Vorschläge machen	Definite and indefinite article: *a/an, the* [ðə/ðɪ] · *this, that, these, those* · Personal pronouns (object form)
	50	Song: Happy birthday		
	51	Text: **The birthday present**		
	52	Exercises		
	56	Summary		
	57	**The time**	Die Uhrzeit angeben	

○ = wahlfrei

Unit	Page	Parts of the unit	Main speech functions	Structures
6	58	Acquisition: British schools; clubs and hobbies	Den Schultag beschreiben; sagen, was man regelmäßig tut; sagen, was jemand nicht tun soll; sich bei jemandem bedanken	Simple present (incl. 3rd person singular) in positive sentences only · Simple present and present progressive: a brief contrast · Negative imperative: *Don't do that, please.*
	62	Text: **New friends**		
	63	Exercises		
	68 ○	Extra Reading: **An interesting job?**		
	70	Summary		
7	71	Acquisition: Rooms and furniture; jobs at home	Das Haus oder die Wohnung beschreiben; sagen, wie oft jemand etwas tut; über die Arbeit im Haus sprechen; sagen, was man mag oder nicht mag	Word order: Subject – Verb – Object · Word order with frequency adverbs: *always, often, usually, sometimes, never* · Simple present in negative sentences · Simple present and present progressive: a further contrast
	74	Text: **The new rooms**		
	75	Exercises		
	80	Summary		
	81	**British money**	Über Geld und Preise reden	
8	82	Acquisition: Pocket-money, free-time activities, sports	Sagen, was jemand regelmäßig oder gerade tut; nach Gewohnheiten fragen; ein Einkaufsgespräch führen	Word order in subordinate clauses and in questions · Simple present in *yes/no*-questions and short answers, questions with question words · Simple present and present progressive: a full contrast
	86	Text: **The record-player**		
	87	Exercises		
	92 ○	Song: My Bonnie		
	93 ○	Extra Reading: **It eats pupils for breakfast**		
	94	Summary		

○ Extra Unit

9	96	Acquisition: Buildings in a town; talking about the place where you live; holidays; sights in Britain	Nach dem Weg fragen; den Weg beschreiben; über den Wohnort sprechen; über Ferien sprechen	
	100	Text: **Come and see Britain**		

○ Extra Page

	102	Quiz about the book

	103	The English alphabet · English sounds · Grammatical terms
	104	Names
	105	Vocabulary
	123	Alphabetical list of words

Introduction

Here's Hatfield.
It's a town in England.
It's near London.

Introduction

Introduction

Activity

And you?

Song: One, two, three, four

Unit 1 A
Jemanden begrüßen; um Auskunft bitten und Auskunft über sich geben

1

Kevin: Good morning. **I'm** Kevin Connor. I'm new here.
Mr Hill: Good morning, Kevin. I'm Mr Hill. I'm your English teacher ... and here's your new class.

→ Ex 1a
(Möglicher Einsatzort für Exercise 1a)

2

Mr Hill: How old are you, Kevin?
Kevin: Eleven.
Mr Hill: And where are you from?
Kevin: I'm from Dover.

Ask a partner.	
You:	*Partner:*
How old are you?	...
Where are you from ?	...

I'm Kevin Connor. = **I am** Kevin Connor.
Here's your new class. = **Here is** your new class.

1A

3 *Sally:* Hallo. **Are you** Kevin Connor?
Kevin: **Yes, I am.** What's your name?
Sally: Sally King.
Kevin: Are you in my class?
Sally: **No, I'm not.** But my brother is in your class.
→ Ex 1b

4 *Dave:* Oh, **you're** here, Kevin. Hallo, Sally.
Sally: Hallo, Dave.
Kevin: Dave, is Sally your sister?
Dave: Yes, that's right.

5 My name is Kevin Connor.
I'm English.
I'm a pupil at Park School.
I'm in class 1F.

 My name is Kerstin Bauer.
I'm not English. I'm German.
I'm a pupil at Goldberg School.
I'm in class 5.

And you?	**Ask a partner.**	
	You:	*Partner:*
My …	What's your name?	…
I'm …	Are you German?	…
I'm not …	How old are you?	…
	Are you in class 5B?	…
	Are you a new pupil?	…
	Where are you from?	…

→ Ex 2–4

What's your name? = **What is** your name?
You're German. = **You are** German.
That's right. = **That is** right.

⚠ **You're** in class 5. **Your** teacher is Herr Schmidt. Are you English? — Yes, I am.
Du bist … **Dein** … *Oder:* — Yes, I'm English.
Aber niemals: Yes, I'm̶.

1A

Auskunft über andere geben

6

tall, lively — *small, lively* — *small, quiet* — *tall, lively*

Dave — Kevin — Liz — Sandra

Dave **is** tall.
Kevin **isn't** tall. **He's** small.
Liz is small, too. And **she's** quiet.
Sandra isn't quiet. She's lively.

Dave is a tall and lively boy.
Liz is a small and quiet girl.
And Kevin? — He's ...
And Sandra? — ...

The rabbit is from Hatfield, too.
It's small and it's very lively.
It's a nice rabbit.

→ S 1a · Ex 5

(Möglicher Einsatzort
für Summary-Abschnitt 1a)

And in your class?

Matthias is ...
And Susanne? — She's ...
She isn't ...

7

| Is | Mr Hill
Sandra
Kevin
your teacher
your brother
your sister | nice?
German?
a teacher?
small?
twelve?
lively?
tall?
quiet? | — Yes, he is./Yes, she is.
— No, he isn't./No, she isn't. |

8 What's his name?/What's her name?

He's tall and he's a teacher. His name is ...
She's small and quiet. Her name is ...
He's from Dover. His ...
Her brother is Dave King. ...
She's tall and lively. ...
He's tall and lively and he's twelve. ...

Kevin Connor
Dave King
Liz Dean
Sandra Bell

Mr Hill
Sally King

He's a boy. = **He is** a boy.
She's a girl. = **She is** a girl.
It's a rabbit. = **It is** a rabbit.

⚠ **He's** tall.   **His** brother is tall.
  Er ist ...   **Sein** Bruder ...

He isn't tall. = **He is not** tall.
She isn't small. = **She is not** small.
It isn't my rabbit. = **It is not** my rabbit.

Auskunft über sich und andere geben   **1A**

9

Kevin is a new pupil at Park School. Dave, Liz and Sandra **are** pupils in the same class. **They're** in class 1F. They're friend**s**. Dave and Kevin are boy**s**, Liz and Sandra are girl**s**. Dave is twelve, but Kevin, Liz and Sandra **aren't** twelve. They're eleven.

Are Dave and Kevin in class 1F? — **Yes, they are.**

Are Dave and Kevin ten? — **No, they aren't.** Dave is twelve, and Kevin is eleven.

Are Liz and Sandra teachers at Park School? — Of course not. They're pupils.

→ S 1b · Ex 6-8

10

 Liz: Sandra Bell and I are friends.
We're at the same school.
We're in the same class.

 Dave: Tom Green and I are friends, too.
We're at the same school.
But **we aren't** in the same class.

→ S 2 · Ex 9

They're boys. = **They are** boys.   They **aren't** girls. = They **are not** girls.
We're pupils. = **We are** pupils.   We **aren't** in the same class. = We **are not** in the same class.

○ **Song: They're in my class at school**

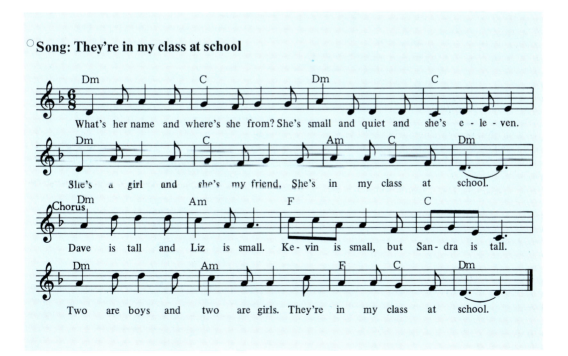

○ wahlfrei

Oh!

Kevin: Here's my teacher.
Tom: Mr Hill?
Kevin: Yes, ssh!

Kevin: Good afternoon, Mr Hill.
Mr Hill: Good afternoon. ... Aren't you the new pupil?
Kevin: Yes, Mr Hill. I'm Kevin Connor. I'm in your class.
Mr Hill: Oh, yes. Of course. You're in my class. You're Kevin. And you're Dave.
Tom: No, I'm not, Mr Hill.
Mr Hill: No? What's your name?
Tom: Tom Green.
Mr Hill: Oh, yes. Tom Green. Of course.
Tom: But I'm not in your class, Mr Hill.
Mr Hill: Oh!

1 Ex

1 Say it in English: *Begrüßung und Verabschiedung*

Begrüßen kann man sich auf Englisch mit	▶ **Hallo.**
Bei Erwachsenen sagt man auch häufig (je nach Tageszeit)	▶ **Good morning, good afternoon, good evening.**
Beim Verabschieden verwendet man Bei Freunden und Bekannten	▶ **Goodbye.** ▶ **Bye.**

a *Was sagen sie?*

Kevin and Dave Liz and Miss Black Dave and Mr Hill Kevin and Sandra

b *Role-play*

Stelle dir vor, du triffst einen Jungen oder ein Mädchen aus England. Begrüßt euch. Fragt euch nach eurem Namen, nach eurem Alter und wo ihr herkommt. Dann verabschiedet euch.

2 *You're new in class 1B at Park School.*

1. Are you new in Hatfield? — Yes, I am.
2. Are you English? — No, ...
3. Are you German? — . . .
4. Are you from Bonn? — . . .
5. Are you a pupil at Park School? — . . .
6. Are you in class 1F? — . . .

3 *Ask questions.*

1. What's — class 1F?
2. How old — you from?
3. Are you a pupil at — your name?
4. Where are — twelve?
5. Are you — Park School?
6. Are you from — are you?
7. Are you in — German?
8. Are you — Mainz?

4 *A new pupil?*

1. Are you new here? — Yes, I'm new here.
2. Are . . . class? — Yes, I'm in your class.
3. What's . . . ? — Heidi Keller.
4. . . . ? — Eleven.
5. . . . ? — No. I'm not from Hamburg.
6. . . . from? — I'm from Stuttgart.

1 Ex

5 *Oh no!*

1. Mr Hill is German. — Oh no! He isn't German. He's English.
2. He's small. — Oh no! He isn't . . . .
3. Liz is tall and lively. — Oh no! She . . . .
4. Dave is a teacher at Park School. — . . .
5. Sandra is twelve. — . . .
6. Liz is from London. — . . .
7. Kevin is in class 2F. — . . .
8. Park School is in Dover. — . . .

6 *Combination exercise*

| Dave and Kevin
Liz and Sandra
Mr Hill and Miss Black | are
aren't | friends.
boys.
girls.
teachers.
brothers.
sisters.
pupils. | ▶ | They're
They aren't | pupils at Park School.
teachers at Goldberg School.
in class 1F.
friends.
boys.
girls.
teachers. |

Dave and Kevin are friends. They're pupils at Park School.
Dave and Kevin aren't . . . . They're . . . .
And Liz and Sandra? And Mr Hill and Miss Black?

7 *Fill in:* **is — are**

Matthias . . . German. He and Martina . . . pupils at Goldberg School. Martina . . . his sister. Matthias . . . in class 5 and Martina . . . in class 6. Matthias and Stefan . . . friends. Stefan . . . in class 6. . . . he and Martina friends, too? Yes, they . . . .

8 *Fill in:* **is** (4×) **isn't** (3×) **He's She's It's are** (4×) **They're they aren't**

Dave and Liz . . . from Hatfield. Kevin . . . new in Hatfield. . . . from Dover. Liz and Sandra . . . in class 1F, but Sally . . . in class 1F. Sandra . . . from Woodside. . . . near Hatfield. Sandra and Liz . . . friends. . . . eleven. Kevin . . . eleven, too. But Dave . . . eleven. Dave and Tom . . . friends, but . . . in the same class. Sandra . . . a lively girl. Liz . . . lively. . . . a very quiet girl.

9 *You and your friend/your brother/your sister*

Schreibe einen ähnlichen Text über dich und einen Jungen oder ein Mädchen. Die folgenden Wörter können dir dabei helfen.

German   English   from . . .
near . . .   pupils at . . . School
in class . . .   the same class   brothers
sisters   friends   ten   eleven
twelve   quiet   lively   tall   small

Thomas and I are German. We're from Bingen. We're pupils at the same school, but we aren't in the same class. I'm in class 5. Thomas and I are brothers. He's twelve and I'm ten.

1 Ex

10 WORDS WORDS WORDS

German: ja und nein   *English:* yes and ...

boys	sister	1. boys and girls
English	evening	2. English and German
brother	lively	3. brother and ...
teacher	German	4. ...
hallo	pupil	5. ...
eleven	goodbye	6. ...
small	girls	7. ...
quiet	tall	8. ...
morning	twelve	9. ...

11

Short *forms:*	Long *forms:*
1. I'm new here.	I am new here.
2. You aren't English.	You are not ....
3. What's your name?	What ...?
4. You're German.	...
5. He's my friend.	...
6. She isn't my sister.	...
7. We're from Hamburg.	...
8. Here's the teacher.	...
9. They're in my class.	...

12 Sounds

[iː] Dean, teacher, he, she ("Dean"-sound)
[ɪ]   in, it, is, sister, English ("in"-sound)
[eɪ] say, name, Dave, same ("say"-sound)
[aɪ] my, goodbye, I, nice, right ("my"-sound)

[v] very, Kevin, lively ("very"-sound)
[w] we, where, quiet ("we"-sound)
[ð] they, the, brother ("they"-sound)
[l] Bell, girl, school ("Bell"-sound)

Dave King is twelve. His sister is nice. His teacher is Mr Hill. Sandra Bell is a tall girl. That's right. My name is Kevin. The rabbit is very small and very lively. We aren't twelve. We're eleven.

Was sage ich, wenn ...	
... ich wissen will, wie etwas auf Englisch heißt?	What's "Katze" in English?
... ich wissen will, wie ein englisches Wort auf Deutsch heißt?	What's "lively" in German? What's the German (word) for "lively"?

1 S

1 Nomen (Nouns)

a

He	She	It			
Dave	Liz	the name →	der Name	– **er**	
my brother	my sister	the school →	die Schule	– **sie**	aber englisch: **it**
the boy	the girl	the rabbit →	das Kaninchen	– **es**	

b

Singular	Plural
one boy	two boy**s**
one girl	two girl**s**
one friend	two friend**s**

Der Plural wird durch das Anfügen von *-s* an den Singular gebildet.

2 Die Personalpronomen und das Verb „sein" (The personal pronouns and the verb "be")

a Aussagesätze mit Langformen

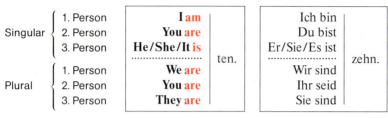

⚠ Oh, you are Mr Hill. = Oh, Sie sind Mr Hill.

b Aussagesätze mit Kurzformen

I am German and you are English. → ein Satz mit Langformen
I'm German and you're English. → ein Satz mit Kurzformen

Wir schreiben Kurzformen, wenn wir gesprochene Sprache schriftlich wiedergeben.

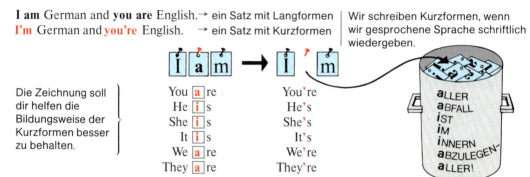

Die Zeichnung soll dir helfen die Bildungsweise der Kurzformen besser zu behalten.

Der erste Buchstabe des zweiten Wortes fällt weg. Der Nagel bleibt. Er heißt „Apostroph".

c Verneinte Sätze

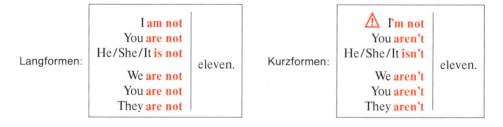

d Fragen und Kurzantworten

⚠ Bei „Ja-Antworten" niemals Kurzformen.

Über die Familie sprechen

Unit 2 A

Friends and families

1. This is Dave King and his family.
   Mr King is Dave**'s** father.
   Mrs King is Dave's mother.
   They're his parents.   → S 2 - Ex 2, 3

Dave (12)   Sally (13)

2. *Dave:* **I've got** a sister. Her name
   is Sally and she's thirteen.
   I haven't got a brother.

Liz (11)   Peter (8)

This is Liz Dean and her family.
Liz: I've got a brother – Peter.
     Peter is . . .
     I haven't got a . . .

This is Kevin Connor and his family.
Kevin: I've got . . .
       Carol is . . . and Tina . . .
       I haven't got a . . .

Kevin (11)   Carol (13)   Tina (10)

Sandra (11)   Wag

And here's Sandra Bell and her mother.
Sandra: I haven't got a brother and I
       haven't got a sister. But I've
       got a dog. His name is Wag.
       He's my best friend.

Quiz: Who is who?

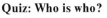

Who is Sally King? – She's Dave King's sister.
Who is Wag? – He's . . .
. . .

And you?
Have you got a brother or a sister?

3. Dave King **has got** a sister. She's thirteen.
   Liz Dean **hasn't got** a sister. But she has got a brother. He's eight.
   Kevin Connor hasn't got a . . . . But he has got . . . . They're . . .

Has	Dave Sandra . . .	got	a brother? two sisters? . . .	— Yes, he has./Yes, she has. — No, he hasn't./No, she hasn't.

→ Ex 4a

> **I've got** a brother. = **I have got** a brother.
> **I haven't got** a sister. = **I have not got** a sister.
> Liz **hasn't got** a sister. = Liz **has not got** a sister.

2 A

Sagen, was jemand besitzt; jemanden vorstellen

4

The Kings in their garden

The Connors on their balcony

The Kings **have got** a house.
They've got a big garden, a garage and a car. Their car is in the garage. Dave and Sally have got a black cat, Susie. They've got a dog, too. His name is Francis.

The Connors **haven't got** a house with a garden. They've got a flat with a balcony. The Connors haven't got a dog or a cat. But Kevin and his sisters have got a small rabbit. → Ex 5

5

Dave King and his new friend, Kevin Connor, are at Dave's house. Mr and Mrs King and Sally are at home, too.

Dave: Mum, this is Kevin. He's in my class at school.
Mrs King: Hallo, Kevin.
Kevin: Hallo, Mrs King. Hallo, Sally.
Dave: Where's Dad?
Mrs King: In the garden with the dog. → Ex 1

6
Kevin: I've got a white rabbit at home. **Have you got** a rabbit?
Dave: **No, we haven't.** But **we've got** a dog and a cat.
Kevin: A dog *and* a cat? Fantastic!
Dave: Yes. Here's **our** cat. She's very old. She's eleven.
Kevin: And your dog?
Dave: Francis? He's young. He's two. Here, Francis!
Francis: Woof, woof! → S 1, 3 · Ex 4b, 6, 7

DOGS ARE TERRIBLE!

They've got a cat. = **They have got** a cat.   They **haven't got** a dog. = They **have not got** a dog.
Where's the dog? = **Where is** the dog?

⚠ **They're** in the garden. **Their** garden is very big.
   Sie sind . . .   Ihr Garten . . .

2 A

7

What's number one in English? — It's a pen. What's number ...? — ...

What's that in English? — It's a book.
— It's a ...

Game:

Teacher: I've got a pen. It's a very nice pen. Have you got a nice pen, too? — Michael.
Michael: Yes, I have. And I've got a book. It's a very nice book. Have you got a nice book, too? — Sabine.
Sabine: No, I haven't. But I've got a bag. It's a very nice bag. Have you got a nice bag, too? — Claudia.

8

THE NUMBERS

1 one [wʌn]	11 eleven [ɪˈlevn]	21 twenty-one [ˈtwentɪˈwʌn]	101 a hundred and one
2 two [tuː]	12 twelve [twelv]	22 twenty-two [ˈtwentɪˈtuː]	150 a hundred and fifty
3 three [θriː]	13 thirteen [ˈθɜːˈtiːn]	30 thirty [ˈθɜːtɪ]	200 two hundred
4 four [fɔː]	14 fourteen [ˈfɔːˈtiːn]	40 forty [ˈfɔːtɪ]	1000 a thousand
5 five [faɪv]	15 fifteen [ˈfɪfˈtiːn]	50 fifty [ˈfɪftɪ]	[əˈθaʊznd]
6 six [sɪks]	16 sixteen [ˈsɪksˈtiːn]	60 sixty [ˈsɪkstɪ]	
7 seven [ˈsevn]	17 seventeen [ˈsevnˈtiːn]	70 seventy [ˈsevntɪ]	
8 eight [eɪt]	18 eighteen [ˈeɪˈtiːn]	80 eighty [ˈeɪtɪ]	
9 nine [naɪn]	19 nineteen [ˈnaɪnˈtiːn]	90 ninety [ˈnaɪntɪ]	
10 ten [ten]	20 twenty [ˈtwentɪ]	100 a hundred [əˈhʌndrəd]	

⚠ three, thirteen, thirty
four, fourteen, forty   *Say:* 13, 14, 15, ... 19 [ˈθɜːˈtiːn, ˈfɔːˈtiːn, ...]
five, fifteen, fifty   *Say:* 30, 40, 50, ... 90 [ˈθɜːtɪ, ˈfɔːtɪ, ...]
a hundred
a hundred **and** ten

Game:

2 Ex

1 **Say it in English:** *sich und andere vorstellen*

So kannst du dich vorstellen	▸ **I'm** Anja (Becker).
So kannst du andere vorstellen	▸ **This is** Jens (and Kerstin).
Das sagst du, wenn du vorgestellt wirst	▸ **Hallo.**
Erwachsene fragen dann oft	▸ **How are you?**
Übliche Antworten auf die Frage, wie es einem geht, sind	▸ **OK, thanks.** ▸ **All right, thank you.**

Role-play

a Einer von euch ist Kevin Connor. Ein zweiter ist sein Freund. Der dritte ist Mr Hill. Kevin begrüßt Mr Hill und stellt seinen Freund vor. Mr Hill fragt den Freund, wie es ihm geht. Der Freund sagt, dass es ihm gut geht.

b Du willst eine Freundin einem Engländer vorstellen. Sage, wie sie heißt und dass sie eine Schülerin in deiner Klasse ist. Der Engländer fragt deine Freundin, wie es ihr geht. Deine Freundin sagt, dass es ihr gut geht.

2 *The Carters and the Whites*

1. Alan Carter is Paul's father. Pat Carter is Paul's mother.
2. Paul is ... brother.
3. Mike White is Susan's ... . Kate White is Susan's ... .
4. Susan and Judy are ... sisters.
5. John is Susan's ... .
6. Judy is ... sister. And Judy is ... sister, too.

2 Ex

3 *Kevin's – Kevin is*

.Kevin. is.. from Dover. .Kevin's. father is Mr Connor. ... eleven. Tina is ... sister.

Sandra's – Sandra is

... from Woodside. Liz is in ... class. ... a nice girl. Mr Hill is ... teacher.

Dave's – Dave is

... from Hatfield. ... Tom's friend. ... tall and lively. Kevin is in ... class.

4 *Brothers and sisters*

a 1. Anne has got a brother. She hasn't got a sister.
   2. Jenny has got ... . She ... .
   3. Judy has got ... and ... .
   4. Karen ... .

Anne →
← Jenny
← Judy →
← Karen

sister   brother

b 1. Have you got a brother or a sister, Anne?
   2. Have you got ... , Jenny?
   3. ... , Judy?
   4. ... ?

   – I've got a brother, but ... .
   – Yes, I have. I've got ... .
   – I've ... .
   – ...

5 *What have they got?*

	The Carters	The Whites	The Browns	The Millers	The Bests
house			✓		✓
garden	✓				
flat	✓	✓		✓	
garage			✓	✓	
balcony		✓			
car				✓	✓
dog	✓				✓
cat		✓			✓
rabbit			✓		

a 1. The Carters haven't got a house. But they've got a flat and a garden.
   2. The Whites ... flat. But they ... a garden or a garage.
   3. The Whites ... a garden. But ... a balcony.
   4. The Browns ... a garage. But ... a car.
   5. The Bests ... a car. But ... a garage.
   6. The Bests ... a house. But ... a garden.
   7. The Carters and the Bests ... dogs.
   8. The Whites and the Bests ... cats. But ... rabbits.
   9. The Browns ... a rabbit. But ... a dog or a cat.
   10. And the Millers?

b *Questions*

   1. Have the Whites got a balcony?
   2. ... the Millers ... house?
   3. ... car?
   4. ... rabbit?
   5. ... cat?

   – Yes, they have. But it's very small.
   – No, they haven't. But they've got a flat and a garage.
   – Yes, they have. But they haven't got a garage.
   – No, they haven't. But they've got a cat and a dog.
   – No, they haven't. But they've got a dog.

6 *That's right...*

1. Jane has got a very lively rabbit. — That's right. Her rabbit is very lively.
2. Paul has got a white cat. — That's right. His ... is ... .
3. We've got a very old dog. — That's right. Our ... .
4. The Carters have got a big garden. — That's right. Their ... .
5. Miss Black has got a terrible dog. — ...
6. The Millers have got a small flat. — ...
7. They have got a German car. — ...
8. Nick has got two terrible sisters. — ...
9. We've got a young German teacher. — ...
10. Susan has got a very nice father. — ...
11. I've got ... . — ... Your ... .

7 *Fill in:* its - your - their - are they - is (2×) - has got - haven't got - I've got - I haven't - Have you got

Anne: *John:*
... a brother, John? — No, ... But ... two sisters.
What are ... names? — Judy and Susan.
How old ... ? — Judy ... eleven and Susan ... thirteen.
 Oh, is this ... dog, Anne?
Yes, his name is Pluto. — We ... a dog, but my sister Judy ... a white
 cat. It's very young.
What's ... name? — Dash.

8 Verflixte Paare! | your — you're | his — he's | its — it's | their — they're |

Diese Paare kann man leicht verwechseln, wenn man nicht aufpasst.
Aber wenn ihr euch den Unterschied gut merkt, kann nichts passieren.
Denkt daran: **Ein** Wort → your, his, its, their (dein, sein, sein, ihr)
 Zwei Wörter → you're, he's, it's, they're (du bist, er ist, es ist, sie sind)

Ein Wort
Have you got **your** pen? (... deinen Füller?)
 His mother is young.
 Its name is Blacky.
Are **their** parents nice?

Zwei Wörter
You're nice. (Du bist nett.)
He's from Hatfield.
It's a nice rabbit.
They're good friends.

Alles klar? — Dann versucht mal diese Sätze:

a His *oder* **he's**? **Their** *oder* **they're**?

1. Dave has got a new pen. It's in .his. pencil-case.
2. The Connors aren't from Hatfield. ... from Dover.
3. Kevin isn't twelve. ... eleven.
4. Dave and Sally have got a dog, Francis. And Susie is ... cat.

b His — he's   its — it's   their — they're   your — you're

1. The Connors have got a flat. .Its. balcony is nice and big. ... very new.
2. Sally King has got a brother. ... name is Dave. ... in Kevin's class.
3. *Mr Hill:* "Oh yes. ... name is Kevin Connor. ... in my class."
4. Kevin and Dave are in the same class. ... in class 1F. ... English teacher is Mr Hill.

2 Ex

9 WORDS WORDS WORDS

a *Three "friends"*

big	colour	Mr	rabbit
biro	dog	Mrs	small
black	father	newspaper	tall
book	magazine	our	their
brother	Miss	pen	white
cat	mother	pencil	your

1. big
   small
   ...
2. biro
   ...
   ...
3. colour
   ...
   ...
4. cat
   ...
   ...
5. book
   ...
   ...
6. brother
   ...
   ...
7. Miss
   ...
   ...
8. our
   ...
   ...

b *Find the partner.*
(Two words have got the same partner.)

1. black and white
2. young and ...
3. tall and ...
4. new and ...
5. mother and ...
6. boys and ...
7. cats and ...
8. brothers and ...
9. teachers and ...

c *Was braucht man*

1. um etwas auszuradieren?   A rubber.
2. um eine gerade Linie zu ziehen?   A ruler
3. um etwas schnell und bequem auszurechnen?   A calculator
4. um Mäuse zu fangen?   A cat
5. um alles Schreibzeug beieinander zu haben?   A pencil-case
6. um Bücher, Hefte usw. in die Schule mitzunehmen?   A bag
7. um etwas zu schreiben, das man ausradieren kann?   A ...
8. um nicht zu Fuß gehen zu müssen?   A bike   *Und was braucht er?*
9. um zu lesen, was es Neues in der Welt gibt?   A magazine   A rabbit, of course!

10 Sounds

[e] **pen**, ten, pencil, twelve, friend
[æ] **bag**, cat, flat, rabbit, fantastic
[ʌ] **mum**, number, brother, colour
[ɑː] **ask**, class, father, car, garden

[ʃ] **she**, short, English, combination
[tʃ] **teacher**, question
[dʒ] **German**, garage, Judy, John
[r] **right**, friend, biro, Peter͜ is, here͜ are

My rabbit and my black cat are best friends. Ten fantastic pens in a black bag.
Ask a short question in English. John and Judy Johnson are German teachers.
My partner͜ and I; her mother͜ and father; a cat or͜ a dog; Dover͜ is in England.
Here͜ are four͜ English girls. Our parents are͜ at home. It's for͜ our͜ old friend Carol.

Was sage ich, wenn ...	
... ich eine Frage habe?	I've got a question.
... ich zu spät komme?	Sorry I'm late.

1 have (got)

a Aussagesätze und verneinte Sätze (Positive and negative sentences)

I **have got**	
You **have got**	
He/She/It **has got**	a balcony.
We **have got**	
You **have got**	
They **have got**	

I **have not got**	
You **have not got**	
He/She/It **has not got**	a garden.
We **have not got**	
You **have not got**	
They **have not got**	

Deutsch: Ich habe einen Balkon.
Du hast einen ... usw.

Ich habe keinen (wörtlich: nicht einen) Garten.
Du hast keinen ... usw.

b Fragen und Kurzantworten (Questions and short answers)

Have I **got**	
Have you **got**	
Has he/she/it **got**	a garden?
Have we **got**	
Have you **got**	
Have they **got**	

	I **have**.		I **haven't**.
	you **have**.		you **haven't**.
Yes,	he/she/it **has**.	No,	he/she/it **hasn't**.
	we **have**.		we **haven't**.
	you **have**.		you **haven't**.
	they **have**.		they **haven't**.

 Bei Kurzantworten kein *got*.

c Langformen und Kurzformen

Long form		Short form
I have got	→	**I've** got
you have got	→	**you've** got
we have got	→	**we've** got
they have got	→	**they've** got

Long form		Short form
have not got	→	**haven't** got
has not got	→	**hasn't** got

In Aussagesätzen mit der 3. Person Singular verwenden wir zunächst nur die Langformen:

he has got, she has got, it has got.

2 Der Genitiv (The possessive form)

Sally is Dave**'s** sister. Dave and Liz are Sandra**'s** friends. This is Kevin Connor**'s** rabbit.

 Kevin**'s** rabbit is white. = Kevins Kaninchen ist weiß. Das **'s** zeigt an, (zu) wem etwas gehört.
It**'s** white. = Es **ist** weiß. ⟶ Hier ist das **'s** die Kurzform von *is*.

3 Die Possessivpronomen (The possessive adjectives)

I am twelve. **My** sister is eleven.
You are eleven. **Your** brother is ten.
He is my friend. **His** name is Tom.
She is my friend. **Her** name is Liz.
It is a school. **Its** name is Park School.

We are in class 1B. **Our** teacher is Miss Black.
You are in class 1F. **Your** teacher is Mr Hill.
They are sisters. **Their** name is Connor.

Unit 3 A

Jemandem sagen, was er tun soll; sagen, was jemand gerade tut

1 It's Saturday morning. It's nine o'clock and the Connors are at home.

Mrs Connor: What time is it, please?
Mr Connor: Nine o'clock.
Mrs Connor: Oh, we're late. Hurry up, Carol.
Carol: OK, Mum.

→ Ex 1

2 Mr Connor, Kevin and Tina are in the garage now. Tina has got a problem with her bike. She has got a puncture.

Tina: Dad, I've got a puncture.
Mr Connor: Well, **repair** it. It's no problem.
Tina: Oh, help me, Dad. Please.
Mr Connor: Sorry, but I've got no time. Kevin, help your sister, please. She has got a puncture.
Kevin: OK, Dad.

→ S 1, 2 · Ex 2

3 It's ten o'clock now.

Tina **is repairing** her puncture.
Kevin is helping his sister.

Mr Connor is working in the garage.
He's painting the garage door.

Mrs Connor is at a paper shop.
She's buying a magazine.

Carol is at a shop, too.
She's buying a cassette.

And Kevin's rabbit? It's at home.
It's playing with the cassette-recorder.

He's painting the door. = **He is painting** the door.
She's buying a book. = **She is buying** a book.
It's playing with the cassette. = **It is playing** with the cassette.

3A

4 Who is doing what?

Mr Connor	is helping	the door.
Sandra	is buying	with the cassettes.
The rabbit	is painting	a magazine.
Mr King	is playing	her bike.
Liz	is repairing	her mother.

Mr Connor is painting the door.
Sandra is ...
...

Who is buying ... ? — Mr King.
Who is ... ? — Kevin's rabbit.
...

→ Ex 3

5

It's eleven o'clock now. Liz Dean and Kevin Connor are at Dave King's house.

Kevin: Good morning, Mrs King. Where's Dave?
Mrs King: Oh, he's in his room.
Kevin: **What's he doing?** His homework?
Mrs King: Of course not. He's watching TV.
Liz: **Is he watching** the tennis match?
Mrs King: **Yes, he is.** And Sally is in the garage, Liz. She's helping her father.

6

What's Dave doing? — He's ...
What's Kevin doing? — He's ...
What's Sandra ... ? — She's ...

Is Dave ... ? — Yes, he is.
  — No, he isn't. He's ...

→ Ex 4, 6

What's he doing? = **What is** he doing?

3 A

7 It's twelve o'clock now. Kevin and Dave are still in Dave's room. **They're reading** magazines. They're listening to Dave's cassettes, too.

Mr King and the two girls are in the garage. Mr King is cleaning the garage.
Liz and Sally **aren't helping** Mr King. They're cleaning and repairing Mrs King's old bike for Sally. Sally's bike is at the repair shop.

Liz and Sally   Mr and Mrs King

Sandra and Mrs Bell   Mr and Mrs Connor   Carol and Tina

→ Ex 5

8 What are Dave and Kevin doing now?
— They're ...

Are Dave and Kevin ... ?
— Yes, they are.
— No, they aren't. They're ...

9

It's one o'clock now. Liz is still at Sally's house. She's on the phone. She's talking to her mother.

Mrs Dean: Liz, it's one o'clock. **What are you doing?**
Liz: **I'm helping** Sally. **We're repairing** her mother's bike.
Mrs Dean: Well, hurry up, please. We're hungry and we're waiting for you.
Liz: OK, Mum.

→ S 3 · Ex 7

They're reading magazines. = **They are reading** magazines.
I'm helping Sally. = **I am helping** Sally.
We're repairing her mother's bike. = **We are repairing** her mother's bike.
Liz and Sally **aren't working** in the garden. = Liz and Sally **are not working** in the garden.

10 It's Saturday afternoon. Dave, Sally, Liz and Sandra are together. They're on their way to the swimming-pool. Here they're talking to Kevin and Carol.

Sally: We're going to the swimming-pool, Kevin. Are you coming?
Kevin: In a minute. I'm repairing my bike.
Sally: Are you coming, too, Carol?
Carol: Sorry. I've got no time.
→ Ex 10

11

Dave, Sally, Kevin, Liz and Sandra are at the swimming-pool now.
The sun is shining. Dave and Sally are swimming. Kevin and Liz are sitting together. They're listening to a cassette. Sandra is doing nothing. She's tired. She's sleeping.

Two boys are playing football.
A man is reading a newspaper.
A woman is . . .
. . .
→ S 3c · Ex 8, 9

Song: Brother John

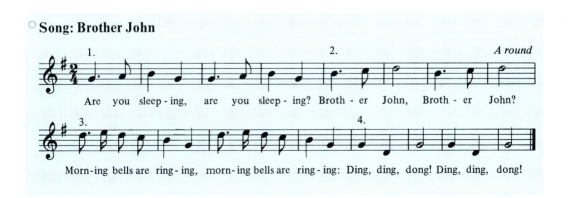

Are you sleep-ing, are you sleep-ing? Broth-er John, Broth-er John?
Morn-ing bells are ring-ing, morn-ing bells are ring-ing: Ding, ding, dong! Ding, ding, dong!

3 T

No problem for Dave?

Liz Dean and Sally King are on their way to the swimming-pool in Potters Park. Dave King is in the garden.

Liz: Hallo, Dave. Sally and I are on our way to
5 Potters Park. Are you coming, too?
Dave: Yes, OK. – But, Sally, are you going on Mum's old bike?
Sally: Yes. It's old but it's still good. And my bike is at the repair shop.
10 *Dave:* But it's ten miles to Potters Park.
Sally: Is that a problem?
Dave: Not for me.

Dave, Liz and Sally are together now.
They are on their way to Potters Park.

15 *Dave:* Hurry up, Sally. We're waiting.
Sally: I'm tired.
Liz: Yes, I'm tired, too.
Dave: Well, I'm not. Bye!

It is ten minutes later.

20 *Liz:* That's nice. Are you waiting for Sally and me?
Dave: No. I've got a puncture.
Sally: Well, repair it. It's no problem.
Dave: Erm, have you got a repair kit?
25 *Sally:* Yes. Here you are, little brother.

Liz and Sally are in Potters Park now. The sun is shining and Liz and Sally are swimming.
But Dave is not with the girls.
30 Where is he?

He is still repairing his puncture.
Dave has got a new bike, but he has got a problem.
Mrs King's bike is old, but ten miles is no problem
35 for Sally.

3 Ex

1 *What time is it, please?*

1. Carol, what time is it, please?
   — It's three o'clock.
   Thank you.

2. Tony, what . . . ?
   — It's . . . .
   Thank . . . .

3. Mr Hill, what . . . ?
   — It's . . . .
   . . .

2 *No problem. Fill in:* a, e, i, o, u

1. Find the rabbit./th- p-nct-r-./th- r-ght w-rd.
2. -sk y--r t--ch-r./- fr--nd./y--r m-th-r./my p-r-nts.
3. H-lp y--r fr--nd./J-hn w-th h-s -x-rc-s-./y--r f-th-r.
4. R-p--r th- c-lc-l-t-r./th- c-r./th- p-nct-r-./S-ndr-'s b-g.

3 *Sandra is helping her mother. And Dave?*

1. Sandra is helping her mother.
2. Dave is . . . ing . . . .
3. Liz is . . . .
4. Sally . . . .
5. Kevin . . . .
6. Tina . . . .
7. Wag . . . .
8. The cat . . . .

4 *Questions. Fill in:* **What's   Where's   Who is**

1. . . . Susan doing? — She's playing.
2. . . . she playing? — In the garden.
3. . . . she playing? — Tennis.
4. . . . Tom doing? — He's working.
5. . . . he working? — In his room.
6. . . . helping Tom? — His friend.

5 *Fill in:* is . . . ing — are . . . ing

Mrs King . . . (work) in the house. Dave . . . (help) his mother. Mr King and Sally . . . (work) in the garage. Mr King . . . (paint) the garage door and Sally . . . (repair) her puncture. Susie and Francis . . . (play) in the garden.

3 Ex

6 *Tom! Tom! Hurry up.*

1. Where's Tom?
   What's he doing?
   What time is it?
   Tom! Tom! Hurry up.
   We're late.

   — He's in the garden.
   — He's playing with his dog.
   — It's three o'clock.

2. ... Jane?
   What's she ... ?
   What time ... ?
   Jane! Jane! Hurry ... .
   We're ... .

   — She's ... her room.
   — ... with her cat.
   — It's ... .

3. ... Bob?
   What's ... ?
   ... time ... ?
   Bob! ... .
   ... late.

   — ... the garage.
   — He's ... .
   — It's ... .

7 *They've got no time.*

Sandra hat mehrere ihrer Freunde angerufen, weil sie mit jemandem spielen will. Warum können sie nicht kommen?

1. *Dave:*   I'm sorry, but ... Dad in the garden.
2. *John:*   Carol is here. ... our homework.
3. *Liz:*   Not now. ... a tennis match.
4. *Tom:*   Sorry, but ... Judy and Martin.
5. *Susan:* Tina and I ... my bike.
6. *Jane:*   I'm sorry, but Kate and Sally are here.
             ... Sally's new cassette.

We're listening to
I'm watching
I'm helping
We're doing
are repairing
I'm waiting for

8 *Find the answers to the questions.*

1. What are the girls doing?   — They're ... .
2. What are the boys doing?   — ...
3. What are the man and the woman doing?   — ...

4. Are the man and the boy buying a TV?   — No, ...
5. What are they buying?   — ...
6. What are the girls buying?   — ...

7. What are the boys doing?   — ...
8. Are the girls helping the boys?   — ...
9. What are they doing?   — ...

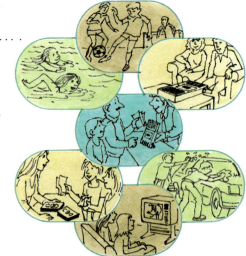

9 *What are they doing?*

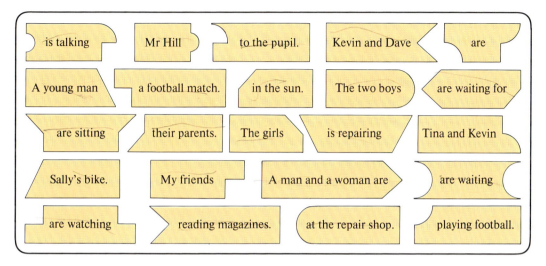

1. A young man . . . . 2. My friends . . . . 3. The girls . . . . 4. The two boys . . . . 5. A man and a woman . . . . 6. Kevin and Dave . . . . 7. Tina and Kevin . . . . 8. Mr Hill . . . .

10 Say it in English: *zustimmen und ablehnen*

Wenn du jemanden fragen willst, ob er/sie mitkommen will, fragst du	▸ **Are you coming?**
Wenn du mitgehen willst, sagst du	▸ **Yes, OK./Yes, all right.**
Wenn du nicht mitgehen kannst, sagst du	▸ **Sorry, I'm busy./Sorry, I've got no time.**
Wenn du mitgehen willst, aber gerade noch mit etwas anderem beschäftigt bist, sagst du	▸ **In a minute.** I'm listening to a cassette.

Are you coming?

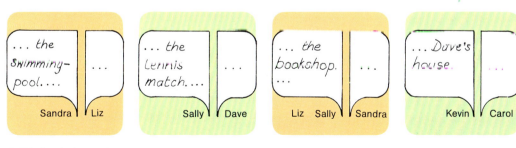

1. Liz hat keine Zeit.
2. Dave kann nicht. Er ist beschäftigt.
3. Sandra will mitgehen.
4. Carol will etwas später mitgehen. Sie liest gerade eine Zeitschrift.

1. *Sandra:* I'm going to the swimming-pool. Are you coming? – *Liz:* Sorry, I've got no time.   *Go on.*

3 Ex

11 WORDS WORDS WORDS

a
Who is it?
A boy or a g...?
A pupil or a t...?
A father or a m...?
A man or a w...?

What is it?
A pen or a p...?
A newspaper or a m...?
A cat or a d...?
A house or a f...?

Where are they?
... school?
... home?
... Sandra's house?
... the balcony?

b *Combination exercise*

a big garage
a small flat
a new pupil
a fantastic game
a good repair shop
a German family
a new bike
a girl on her way

with a balcony
at my school
with a puncture
to school
for bikes
for boys and girls
for three cars
with a boy and two girls

c In English, please.

Was sagst du, wenn du willst, dass

1. Tom sich beeilt? — Hurry up, Tom.
2. Liz einen Moment wartet? — ... a minute, Liz.
3. Jane mit ihrem Lehrer redet? — ...
4. Dave sich das Fußballspiel ansieht? — ...
5. Kevin seinen Lehrer fragt? — ...
6. Judy sich deine neue Cassette anhört? — ...
7. Sandra still ist? — ...
8. John seine neue Cassette vorspielt? — ...
9. Susan ihre Hausaufgaben macht? — ...

12 Sounds

[əʊ] **Oh**, n**o**, g**o**, h**o**me, ph**o**ne, D**o**ver, **O**K
[aʊ] n**ow**, h**ow**, t**ow**n, **ou**r, h**ou**se
[ŋ] s**o**ng, l**o**ng, morn**ing**, is read**ing**, is paint**ing**, is work**ing**, is sitt**ing**, is com**ing**

[p] **p**ark, **p**aper, **p**lease, sho**p**, hurry u**p**
[b] **b**ig, **b**e, **b**ook, foot**b**all, ru**bb**er, ra**bb**it

How old is our house? Buy a new felt-tip and a biro, please. Mrs Bell is buying a paper and a book at the shop. The boys and girls are playing football at the swimming-pool. Peter is painting his old bike. I'm not sleeping, I'm reading.

13 Listening comprehension: A nice brother

Was sage ich, wenn ...	
... ich die Hausaufgabe(n) wissen will?	What's for homework, please?
... ich wissen will, auf welcher Seite (im Buch) wir sind?	What page are we on, please?
... ich wissen will, ob etwas richtig ist?	Is this right: "...?" / "...". Is that right?

Das Verb (The verb)

Von jedem englischen Verb gibt es mehrere Formen. Drei lernst du in dieser Unit kennen.

1 Der Infinitiv (The infinitive)

Der Infinitiv ist die Grundform eines Verbs.
Im Deutschen endet der Infinitiv meist auf -en: frag*en*, helf*en*, reparier*en*; sein.
Im Englischen gibt es keine besondere Endung für den Infinitiv: *(to) ask, (to) help, (to) repair, (to) be.*

2 Der Imperativ (The imperative)

Im Englischen hat der Imperativ immer die gleiche Form wie der Infinitiv (aber ohne *to*):
  ask = frag(e), fragt, fragen Sie!
  help = hilf, helft, helfen Sie!
repair = reparier(e), repariert, reparieren Sie!
  be = sei, seid, seien Sie!

Der Imperativ wird verwendet, um jemanden aufzufordern, etwas zu tun, oder um Befehle zu geben, z.B.
Ask your partner. Help your sister, please. Be quiet.
Nach Imperativsätzen steht meistens ein Punkt (kein Ausrufezeichen wie im Deutschen).

3 Die Verlaufsform des Präsens (The present progressive)

Mit *I'm playing* drückst du aus, dass du im Augenblick/gerade spielst. Im Deutschen gibt es keine Verlaufsform. Aber in manchen Gegenden sagt man: „Stör ihn nicht, er ist am (oder: beim) Arbeiten."
„Er ist am/beim Arbeiten." oder „Er arbeitet im Augenblick/gerade." = *He's working.*

a

Positive sentences	
I'**m** You'**re** He'**s**/She'**s**/It'**s** We'**re** You'**re** They'**re**	play**ing**.

Negative sentences	
I'**m not** You **aren't** He/She/It **isn't** We **aren't** You **aren't** They **aren't**	work**ing**.

b

Questions
Are you work**ing**?   **Is** she work**ing**?   **Are** they work**ing**?

Short answers
Yes, I **am**.   No, she **isn't**.   Yes, they **are**.

c Das *present progressive* wird mit einer Form von *be (am/is/are)* + *-ing form* gebildet.
Die *-ing form* wird durch Anfügen von *-ing* an den Infinitiv gebildet:

help → help**ing**   ⚠ Aber: sit → si**tt**ing   come → com**ing**
ask → ask**ing**   swim → swi**mm**ing   shine → shin**ing**
buy → buy**ing**

Unit 4 A

Fragen, ob man etwas haben kann; beschreiben, was vorhanden ist

1 Lots of young people have got pets. Liz Dean's friends have all got pets.

Kevin Connor has got a rabbit.   Dave and Sally King have got a dog and a cat.   Sandra Bell has got a dog.

2 *Liz:* Can we have a pet, Mum? Please?
Mrs Dean: Liz, the house is very small. It's too small for a pet.
Liz: But the Connors have got a flat, and they've got a pet.
Peter: Can't we have a small pet – a rabbit or a hamster?
Mrs Dean: Well, all right. But ask your father tonight. → Ex 1

3 There's a small pet shop in Sandfield Street. Its owner is Mr Singh. He's a lively old man from India and he has got lots of pets. Liz and Peter are looking at the pets in Mr Singh's window.

There's a dog in the window.
There's a budgie.
There's a ...

There are some baskets in the shop.
There are some rabbits.
There are some ... → S 1 · Ex 2-5

And you?
Have you got a pet?
What is it?
What's his/her name?

There's a dog. = There is a dog.

Fragen, ob man etwas tun darf; sagen, was jemand tun muss

4

Liz and Peter are in the shop now.

Mr. Singh: Good afternoon. Can I help you?
Liz: Yes. **May we look** at your pets, please?
Mr Singh: Of course. There are some hamsters, mice and rabbits here. And there are some dogs and cats near the window.

Liz: Oh, here's a nice dog.
Mr Singh: Yes, it's new in the shop.
Liz: It's very nice. **May I touch** it?
Mr Singh: Yes, of course.
→ S 2b · Ex 6, 8

5 *Mr Singh:* A dog is a nice pet, but you **must clean** it. You must feed it. And you must take it for a walk. Every day!

→ S 2c · Ex 7

6 *Liz:* OK. I can take it for a walk on Monday and Tuesday. You can take it for a walk on Wednesday, Thursday and Friday.
Peter: Oh no. It's my turn on Monday and Tuesday, and it's your turn on Wednesday, Thursday and Friday.
Liz: And it's Mum's turn on Saturday and Dad's turn on Sunday.

7 *Peter:* What have you got here, Mr Singh?
Mr Singh: Oh, a big animal from India. Can't you hear it?
Peter: Yes, but I can't see it.
Mr Singh: Well, open the box, but be careful. It's very big.

Peter: Help! What is it?
Mr Singh is laughing.
Mr Singh: Oh, it's only a cassette-recorder. But it's very funny. It's my favourite animal.
Liz: Well, goodbye, Mr Singh. We must talk to our parents now.

4 A

Sagen, was jemand kann

8 What **can** animals **do**?

Some can bark.

Some can sing.

Some can climb trees.

Some can fly — and not only birds.

And some are very clever. They can carry things . . . or catch things.

9 What can animals do? And what **can't** they **do**?

A dog can bark, but it can't fly.
A budgie can fly, but it can't . . .
A cat . . .

→ S 2 · Ex 9, 10

> **And you?**
>
> What can your pet do?

10 Poor Peanut. He's a little dog in a box in a pet shop. He's sleeping now, but in his dreams . . .

He's big and strong.

He can swim across the sea.

He can speak French and Japanese.

He can lift his box.

He can carry ten bags . . .

. . . and twenty newspapers.

He can do everything. But where's a nice owner for Peanut? He hasn't got a home, only his box in Mr Singh's window.

> A dog **can't** sing. = A dog **cannot** sing.

○ **Song: My friend Jack**

4 T

A wet afternoon

It is Thursday evening and Mr Dean is at home.

Liz: Dad, there's a very nice dog in the pet shop. His name is Peanut and he hasn't got a home.
Peter: And we haven't got a pet.
Mr Dean: No dogs. Not in our house.
Liz: Oh, please, Dad. Please. You can't say "No".
Peter: He's very clever, Dad. He can carry your newspaper.
Mr Dean: And he can bark, too. No, thank you.
Liz and Peter: Oh, Dad. *Please.*
Mr Dean: All right. But listen. He's *your* dog and not my dog. You must clean Peanut. You must feed Peanut, and you must take Peanut for a walk every day.
Liz: Yes, all right. It's my turn on Monday, Wednesday and Friday morning. And it's Peter's turn on Tuesday, Thursday and Friday afternoon.
Mr Dean: And on Saturday and Sunday?
Peter: It's your turn, Dad.
Mr Dean: Oh no, it isn't.

It is Sunday afternoon and Peanut has got a new home with Liz and Peter. They must take Peanut for a walk every day, of course, but now it is raining ...

Mr Dean: Hey, you two. It's five o'clock. Take Peanut for a walk, please.
Peter: Liz, it's your turn.
Liz: What, again?
Mr Dean: Hurry up. He's your dog.
Liz: But it's raining. It's too wet.

It is six o'clock now.

Mr Dean: Liz, Peter. Peanut is barking.
Peter: Hurry up, Liz. It's your turn.
Liz: All right, all right. In a minute. I'm watching TV.
Mr Dean: Liz, Peanut is waiting. Hurry up, please.
Liz: Can't I wait, Dad? It's still wet.
Mr Dean: Yes, it's *very* wet now.

Right or wrong?

(Lines 1-33): 1. It's Tuesday. — That's wrong. It's Thursday. 2. Liz and Peter are at home. — That's right. 3. Liz and Peter have got a dog. 4. Peanut is in the pet shop. 5. Peter and Liz must take Peanut for a walk every week.
(Lines 34-42): 6. It's Sunday morning now. 7. Peanut is with the Deans. 8. The sun is shining.
(Lines 43-49): 9. Peanut is sleeping. 10. It's Peter's turn. 11. It's wet.

→ Ex 11

4 Ex

1 *Can I have ...?*

1. I haven't got my repair kit with me. Can I have your repair kit, please?
   — Yes, of course. Thank you.
2. I haven't got ... with me. Can I ..., please?
   — No, I'm sorry.
3. I ... . Can ... ?
   — Yes, ...
4. I ... . ?
   — No, ...

2 *Look at the pictures.*
There's ... . There are ... .

1. There's a ... in the ... .
2. There are some ... in ... .

Go on.

3 *What pets are there in the window?*

1. There's a hamster in the window. It's ... a box.
2. There are some ... in the window. They're ... .
3. ... two ... .
4. ... a black ... . It's ... .
5. ... some young ... .

4 *Fill in:* **there are   they're   their**

1. Where are my cassettes?
   — ... in my bag.
   ... some books in your bag, but no cassettes.
2. ... two girls in the garden. Are they Sandra's friends?
   — Yes. ... from Woodside, too.
3. Mrs Bell can't find the newspaper.
   — ... some newspapers in Wag's basket.
4. What are you doing here?
   — I'm waiting for my parents. ... late. Isn't that ... car?
5. Where are Liz and Peter?
   — ... at the pet shop. ... looking at Mr Singh's dogs.
6. Are Dave and Sally at home? ... bikes aren't in the garage.
   — No, ... on ... way to the swimming-pool.

4 Ex

5 *Plurals:* [-s] *or* [-z] *or* [-ɪz] ?

bike, owner, budgie, garage, boy, garden, house, cassette, mile, pet shop, box, window, game, newspaper, match, flat, family, town, pencil-case, book, dog, rabbit, teacher, felt-tip, class, name, pupil, basket, cage

[-s]	[-z]	[-ɪz]
bikes …	owners budgies …	garages …

Go on.

And what's the plural of mouse?

6 *May I … ?*

Combination exercise

1. May I ask — at your pets?
2. … go — a question, please?
3. … touch — your newspaper?
4. … listen — to the swimming-pool?
5. … have — the football match?
6. … look — near the window?
7. … watch — to your new cassette?
8. … sit — your dog?

7 *Dave's friends have got no time.*

Fill in: must *and* a, e, i, o, u.

1. Kevin must d- h-s h-m-w-rk.
2. Jane … cl--n h-r r--m.
3. Sandra … t-k- W-g f-r - w-lk.
4. Bob … p--nt - b-x.
5. Carol … h-lp h-r f-th-r.
6. Jill … b-y - n-w c-g-.
7. Tina … w--t f-r K-v-n.
8. Tom … w-rk -n th- g-rd-n.

8 Say it in English: *um Erlaubnis bitten*

Wenn du etwas haben oder tun möchtest, sagst du	▸ **Can** I have your book, **please**? ▸ **May** I touch the dog, **please**?
Als Antwort darauf sagt man	▸ **Yes, of course.** ▸ **Yes, OK./Yes, all right.** ▸ **No, I'm sorry.**

Work with a partner.

a Frage deinen Partner/deine Partnerin, ob du seinen/ihren Bleistift (Lineal/Taschenrechner/ Radiergummi/…) haben kannst.

b Einer von euch ist der Besitzer einer Tierhandlung. Der andere möchte wissen, ob er die Tiere anschauen kann, ob er die Katzen anfassen darf und ob er mit dem jungen Kaninchen spielen kann.

9 *Can rabbits sing?*

| Can | hamsters
rabbits
budgies
dogs
cats
mice | climb trees?
sing?
talk?
swim?
fly?
bark?
catch mice?
carry things? | Of course they can.
Of course not. |

10 *What can that be? – Who can that be? Fill in:* **there's   there are   can't be   must be**

1. Look, Peter, ... a hamster in the shop window.
   – It ... a hamster. It's too small for a hamster.
   It ... a mouse.
2. Look, Anne, ... a girl on the balcony.
   – That ... Jane.
   Oh no, it ... Jane. It ... her sister. Jane is at school.
3. Listen, Tom, ... some mice in the garden.
   – That ... mice. Mice can't bark. It ... a dog.
4. Listen, Mary, ... some budgies in Tom's room.
   – Oh no! That ... budgies. It ... Tom's old cassette-recorder. Tom is repairing it.

11 *Look at "A wet afternoon" on page 40 again. – Now try this:*

Tina: Dad, there's a very ... ... in the ... shop.
            His ... is Billy and he hasn't got a ... .
Mr Connor: No ... ! Not in our ... .
Tina: Oh, please, Dad. You ... say "No".
Mr Connor: Oh yes I can.
Tina: He's very ... , Dad. He can ... .
            He can ... his name.
Mr Connor: Yes, and he can ... , too. No, thank you!

12 WORDS WORDS WORDS

a *Find the hidden plural words. There are seven words in number 1.*

1. FROBBIRDSSUNDOGSTICHAMSTERSOLDFRIDANIMALSANGERFRIENDSUBROOMSASTURNHOMESTER (7)
2. TREPETSMORCATSWENDOOFRABBITSNIBASKETSOUSHOPSAMILFELT–TIPSSORDYBOOKSLEEBERS (7)
3. FRENDDAYSATRURBOYSUNDERBIROSWOBUDGIESMOUSFAMILIESMALKYBALCONIESLNUISERANCE (6)
4. FRAMAGAZINESRAQUESTIONSNUGAMESAMILESUPPUPILSEPPENCILSIDOORSTADTREESWINDOWS (9)
5. FLICAGESTIGARAGESALBOXESUHOUSESYCLASSESLATPENCIL–CASESOMMATCHESTERBUDGYROB (7)

b **The answers in English, please, too.**

1. Where are Liz and Kate?
2. I'm sorry, but I can't come on Saturday.
3. Have you got a pen, please?
4. Listen. That's the phone.
5. Take the dog for a walk, please.
6. *Pet shop owner:* Can I help you?
7. May I feed your dog?
8. A basket in a shop window isn't a nice home for a dog.

– Sie sind noch zu Hause.
– Kannst du am Sonntag kommen?
– Ja, bitte sehr.
– Wer kann das sein?
– Ich bin nicht an der Reihe.
– Ja, darf ich bitte Ihre Hamster sehen?
– Ja, aber sei vorsichtig!
– Natürlich nicht!

13 **Revision:** *mothers or mother's?*

1. Sally is cleaning her ... bike. – Parents is a word for ... and fathers. (mother)
2. There are lots of ... in Mr Singh's window. – My ... name is Henry. (hamster)
3. Are all ... terrible? – Of course not! – Who is your ... best friend? (sister)
4. Sandra has got lots of ... . – My ... bike is old but it's still good. (friend)
5. Our ... English is very good. – But not all ... can speak good English. (teacher)

14 Revision: his *or* he's?

Mr Singh has got a pet shop. … a nice old man from India. … very lively. … pet shop is in Sandfield Street. He has got lots of pets in … shop. … favourite is a tiger in a cassette-recorder! In … window there is a quiet little dog. … name is Peanut. … new in the pet shop. … sleeping now. But in … dreams he has got a new home. … new owners are Liz and Peter Dean.

15 ━━━━━━━━━━━ Sounds ━━━━━━━━━━━

a [-g] do**g**, ba**g**, bi**g**
[-k] boo**k**, tal**k**, bi**k**e, Mi**k**e, bla**ck**
A big dog; a black dog; a big black dog; a black bike and a black bag.

[-d] **d**a**d**, goo**d**, wor**d**, rea**d**
[-t] **c**a**t**, no**t**, shor**t**, fla**t**
Not good; a short word; a good flat; feed the cat; a pet for Dad; read the word.

b [-s] book**s**, pet**s**, bike**s**, shop**s**, basket**s**, rabbit**s**, Miss Black'**s** pet, Mike'**s** cat, Pat'**s** bike; What'**s** your name? It'**s** nice.
[-z] bag**s**, pen**s**, dog**s**, hamster**s**, room**s**, car**s**, sister**s**, Dave'**s** bike, he'**s** nice; Where'**s** Kevin? How'**s** Carol? She'**s** English. He'**s** German.
[-ɪz] box**es**, garage**s**, cage**s**, pencil-case**s**, house**s**, class**es**, match**es**, Liz'**s** biro, Mr**s** Connor

Was sage ich, wenn …	
…ich etwas wiederholt haben möchte?	Can you say that again, please?
…ich etwas auf Deutsch erklärt haben möchte?	Can you explain that in German, please?
…ich zur Toilette gehen möchte?	Can / May I go to the toilet, please?

Just for fun

A rhyme
Is it raining? You can say:

Rain, rain, go away,
Come again another day.

A cat puzzle
Big or small? Black or white? Young or old?

Mr Waggle's cat is small, young and white.
Mr Weggle's cat is small, not young and not black.
Mr Wiggle's cat is not small, not young and black.
Mr Woggle's cat is big, young and not white.
Mr Wuggle's cat is not big, not old, and not black.

Two cats are the same. Can you find the two?

What am I?
Here are my letters:
One is in car, but not in cat,
Two is in bag, and in man and flat.
Three and four are the same letter,
They aren't in ruler, but are in rubber.
Five is in biro, but not in board,
Six is in tall, but not in small.

What am I?

JUNIOR W🌐RLD MAGAZINE

What are your favourite pets?

A good pet

My sister has got a goldfish. A goldfish is a very good pet. Dogs can bark and they can carry things, too. But you can sit and watch a goldfish.

Tina Connor (10)
Hatfield

But you can't take a goldfish for a walk!

A lazy cat

My brother and I have got two pets — a dog and a cat. Our dog is young and lively, but our cat is very old. Susie can still catch mice, but she's too lazy!

Sally King (13)
Hatfield

It's a pity

Dogs are my favourite pets. They're good friends. You can play with dogs. We've got a new dog. His name is Peanut. He's a good dog, but he can't sleep in my room. He must sleep in the garden. It's a pity.

Liz Dean (11)
Hatfield

Miaow!

We've got a cat. Our cat is four. Her name is Tabby. She's very nice. She can understand her name. Tabby can catch mice. There isn't a mouse in the house!

John Hooley (11)
Belfast

She can understand her name . . .

Mary and Rumpelstiltskin

Rumpel . . . who?

My favourite pet is our budgie. We've got a flat, and small birds are good pets for flats. Our budgie can say "Good morning" and "Goodbye", but it can't say its name. It's "Rumpelstiltskin".

Mary Brown (10)
Manchester

And you?

What's your favourite pet?
Write a letter to Junior World Magazine.

4 S

1 Nomen im Plural (Nouns in the plural)

Singular			Plural		
one boy	[-ɔɪ]	Stimmhafte Auslaute	two boys	[-ɔɪz]	
girl	[-l]		girls	[-lz]	
dog	[-g]		dogs	[-gz]	
town	[-n]		towns	[-nz]	
shop	[-p]	Stimmlose Auslaute	shops	[-ps]	
flat	[-t]		flats	[-ts]	
book	[-k]		books	[-ks]	
class	[-s]	Zischlaute	classes	[-sɪz]	
match	[-tʃ]		matches	[-tʃɪz]	
cage	[-dʒ]		cages	[-dʒɪz]	
exercise	[-z]		exercises	[-zɪz]	

Aber: house [-s] houses [-zɪz]

[-z]

[-s]

[-ɪz]

⚠ Bei *-y* am Ende: fami**ly** – fami**lies**, balco**ny** – balco**nies**, aber: b**oy** – b**oys**, d**ay** – d**ays**

Außerdem gibt es ganz unregelmäßige Pluralformen. Einige kennst du schon:
one man, two **men**; one woman [ˈwʊmən], two **women** [ˈwɪmɪn]; one mouse, two **mice**.

2 Can, may, must

Can, may, must sind Hilfsverben (auxiliaries). In Aussagesätzen stehen sie immer zusammen mit dem Infinitiv eines Vollverbs. Im Gegensatz zum Deutschen kann das Vollverb nicht weggelassen werden, z.B. Ich kann Englisch (sprechen). → *I can speak English.*
Beachte die Wortstellung:

Tina **can repair** a bike.   We **must wait** for Liz.

Tina **kann** ein Fahrrad **reparieren.**   Wir **müssen** auf Liz **warten.**

a **can** (können, dürfen)

I / You / He/She/It / We / You / They	**can** swim. [kən]

I / You / He/She/It / We / You / They	**can't** sing. [kɑːnt]

⚠ Die Langform von *can't* heißt:
cannot [ˈkænɒt]

Can I/you/we **have** a pet? — Yes, you can [kæn]./Yes, of course./No, I'm sorry.

b **may** (dürfen)

So kannst du besonders höflich um Erlaubnis bitten:

May I/we **watch** TV now, please? — Yes, all right./No, not now, please.

c **must** (müssen)

I **must take** my dog for a walk. Tina **must help** her father. The tall man **must be** Mr Hill.
Must you **do** your homework now? — Yes, I'm sorry./No, not now.

Das Datum angeben

The calendar

   Make a calendar:

1 There are twelve months in a year:

2 There can be 31 days in a month:

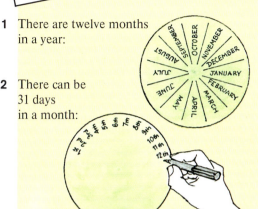

1st first	8th eighth	15th fifteenth
2nd second	9th ninth	20th twentieth
3rd third	10th tenth	21st twenty-first
4th fourth	11th eleventh	22nd twenty-second
5th fifth	12th twelfth	23rd twenty-third
6th sixth	13th thirteenth	30th thirtieth
7th seventh	14th fourteenth	31st thirty-first

3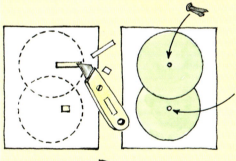

4

What date is it? – It's ...

We write: October 7th, 1989.
We say: October *the* seventh, nineteen eighty-nine.

5 There are four seasons in a year:

spring   summer

autumn   winter

When is spring? – It's in March, April ...
When is summer? – It's in ...
...

Is November in the summer?
– Of course not. It's in the autumn.
Is January in the spring? – ...
...

6

	MAY					
MON	TUES	WED	THU	FRI	SAT	SUN
1	2	3	4	5	6	7
8	9	10	11	12	13	14
15	16	17	18	19	20	21

What day is it today?   – Thursday.
What date is it today?   – May 4th.
What day is it tomorrow?   – Friday.
What date is it next Monday? ...
Go on.

7 **The "how many" game**

How many months are there in 3 years
         weeks are there in 4 years
         days are there in the year 2000
                       February 1988
                       March 1999
                       April 2001

699   31   365   24   29   27   366   77   204

Welche Zahl kommt heraus, wenn man die sechs Lösungen addiert?

Unit 5 A

Über Geburtstage sprechen; Vorschläge machen

1 Birthdays

Dave's birthday is in June.
It's on June 1st.
Sally's birthday is in . . .
It's on . . .
. . .

Ask a partner.

When's your birthday? It's in . . ./on . . .
When's your father's/mother's/. . .'s birthday?

→ Ex 1-3

2

Sandra Bell's birthday is on March 24th.
That's a Saturday, so her birthday party is at the weekend.
Her friends have all got **an i**nvitation to her party.

Activity

Make invitations for your party.

→ S 1 · Ex 4

3
Kevin: Have you got an invitation to Sandra's party, too?
Dave: Yes. Let's go together.
Kevin: OK.
Dave: We must take a present. Why not buy a present together, too?
Kevin: Good idea. What can we buy?
Dave: Well, she's crazy about Mike Walker. Let's buy his new record "Tomorrow isn't today".
Kevin: Yes, OK.

→ Ex 6

---

a birthday party – a**n i**nvitation
the **b**irthday party – the **i**nvitation
[ðə]   [ðɪ]

When's your birthday? = **When is** your birthday?
Let's go. = **Let us** go.

5A

4

Sandra is from Woodside. Woodside is a village near Hatfield. It isn't very big. There are some farms and new houses, but there's only one shop. The owner is Mrs Kent.

5 Today is March 24th. It's Sandra's birthday and her party is in the afternoon. Sandra is in the shop. She's buying some drinks, some biscuits and some crisps.

Sandra has got five bottles of lemonade, six bottles of orange juice, six packets of biscuits and ten packets of crisps.

6 Now Sandra is at home. She's preparing the food for her party.
She's making some sandwiches.

Mrs Bell is helping Sandra. She's making some cakes.

7

Now everything is on the table. There are plates of sandwiches and cakes. There's a tin of biscuits. There are bottles of lemonade and orange juice, and there are packets of crisps.

→ Ex 5

5 A

8 It's Saturday afternoon now and Sandra is looking at her presents.

This radio is from my mum.

That poster is a present from my Aunt Mary.

These cassettes are from my Uncle John.

And **those** two **hamsters** are from my grandfather and grandmother.

→ S 2 · Ex 7, 8

9 Now Sandra is waiting for her guests.

Mrs Bell: Sandra! Tom and his brother are on the phone. Can you come, please?
Sandra (on phone): Hallo. Tom? — Sssh, Mum, I can't hear **him**.
Tom: Hallo, Sandra. Can you hear **me**?
Sandra: Yes, I can hear **you** now. Go on.
Tom: We've got a problem. Can your mum fetch **us**, please, because Dad's car has got a puncture.
Sandra: Well, I can ask **her**. — Mum, Mr Green has got a puncture. Tom and Terry can't come. Can you fetch **them** in the car, please?
Mrs Bell: OK. I'm on my way.
Sandra: No problem, Tom. Mum is on her way.
Tom: Great. See you soon, Sandra. Bye.
Sandra: Bye, Tom.

→ S 3 · Ex 9-11

Song: Happy birthday

Hap - py birth - day to you. Hap - py birth - day to you. Hap - py birth - day dear San - dra, Hap - py birth - day to you.

The birthday present

It is Saturday afternoon and Sandra's guests are at the party. Dave and Kevin are there, too. They have got a present for her.

Kevin: Happy birthday, Sandra. This is for you.
Sandra: For me? That's nice.
Dave: Well, open it.
Sandra: Hey, a record. And it's Mike Walker. He's my favourite singer. Thanks, Kevin. Thanks, Dave.
Dave: You're welcome. Where's the food?
Sally: Oh, Dave!

Sandra: Let's listen to my new record now.
Liz: But it's three o'clock.
Sally: The Dave Sales Pop Shop is on the radio. Let's listen to that.
Sandra: I can listen to Dave Sales every day. Let's play the record. It's a present from Dave and Kevin.
Liz: But it's a fantastic programme, Sandra.
Sally: And there are some great records.
Sandra: No, let's play this record. It's my record-player and it's my birthday.
Liz: It's your birthday, but we're guests here.
Sally: That's right ... Here's Dave Sales now. Listen.

... fantastic record. The next record is for Sandra Bell in Woodside. It's from Liz Dean, Sally King and all her friends at Park School. Happy birthday, Sandra! And here's the record: Mike Walker with "Tomorrow isn't today." ...

(Lines 1-11): 1. Is it Kevin's birthday? 2. What have Dave and Kevin got? 3. What's their present?
(Lines 12-31): 4. What time is it now? 5. What's on the radio? 6. What's the next record on the Dave Sales Pop Shop?

→ Ex 13

5 Ex

1

a *What date is it today?*

1. It's Monday, December 6th.
2. It's Friday, ...
3. It's .... *Go on.*

b *What day is it tomorrow?*

1. It's Tuesday tomorrow.
2. It's ... tomorrow.
3. It's .... *Go on.*

2 *The twelve months in the year*

Schreibe nur die Monatsnamen auf, die im Englischen anders als im Deutschen geschrieben werden! Unterstreiche, was anders ist!

1. <u>J</u>anuary   2. ...

3 *Find the missing word.*

1. spring	summer	...	winter	4. first	second	...	fourth
2. sixth	seventh	...	ninth	5. ninth	tenth	eleventh	...
3. Monday	Tuesday	...	Thursday	6. day	week	...	year

4 *Fill in:* "**a**" *or* "**an**"

... house   ... French car   ... invitation to the party
... owner   ... English town   ... activity for boys and girls
... hamster   ... new owner   ... good friend from England
... pet shop   ... old calculator   ... answer to the question
... animal   ... clever animal   ... nice owner for Peanut

5 *Everything is on the table.*

There's a plate of ....
There are two ... of ....
There .... *Go on.*

6 Say it in English: *Vorschläge machen*

> Vorschläge werden im Englischen häufig so gemacht:
> **Let's** buy a present together. **Why not** ask Dave?
>
> Wenn man einem Vorschlag zustimmt, sagt man:
> **Good idea. Great. OK. All right.**
>
> Eine Ablehnung kann entweder ganz direkt sein:
> **That's silly. That's a silly idea. Oh, no.**
>
> — oder eher höflich formuliert werden:
> **I'm sorry, but I can't. Sorry, but I must** do my homework.
>
> — oder einen Gegenvorschlag enthalten:
> **No, let's** buy a cassette. **Can't we** go on Friday?

What are they saying? Work with a partner.

   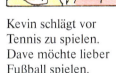 

Dave schlägt vor einige Platten anzuhören. Sally ist damit einverstanden.

Liz schlägt vor fernzusehen, aber Peter findet diese Idee albern.

Kevin schlägt vor Tennis zu spielen. Dave möchte lieber Fußball spielen.

Sally schlägt vor die Tiere anzuschauen. Liz muss aber ihre Hausaufgaben machen.

7 This — these is — are

1. ... girl ... my best friend.
2. ... animals ... very clever.
3. ... box ... too small for the dog.
4. ... ... white mice. They aren't hamsters.
5. ... budgie ... a present from Tim's aunt.
6. ... tennis book ... a present, too.
7. ... big cat ... from India.
8. ... present ... from Uncle George.
9. ... drinks ... for your party.
10. ... table ... too small for ten.

8 That — those isn't — aren't

1. ... car ... English.
2. ... bikes ... French.
3. ... radio ... very old.
4. ... cassette ... Jane's present.
5. ... records ... for Peter.
6. ... garage ... too small.
7. ... party ... next Saturday.
8. ... magazines ... very old.
9. ... farm ... near here.
10. ... birds ... too big for ... cage.

9 Puzzle

Find the missing letters.

1. It's a present from her.
   (my -un-)
2. Let's look at them.
   (the pr-s-nts)
3. Can you carry them?
   (--ose -oxes)
4. We're waiting for him.
   (o-r g--st)
5. Sandra is preparing it.
   (the -oo- for the -ar-y)
6. Who can help us?
   (m- u-cle -nd m-)

10 Him her it them

Complete these sentences.

1. Can you ask . . . ?	(that girl)
2. Can Uncle George fetch . . . ?	(Dave)
3. I can't read	(this sentence)
4. Can I have . . . , please?	(the magazines)
5. Bill can carry	(the basket)
6. May I talk to . . . ?	(Mrs Bell)
7. Catch	(the mouse)
8. Look at	(the presents)
9. Who is coming with . . . ?	(Liz)
10. Who is making . . . ?	(the cakes)
11. Are you waiting for . . . ?	(Tom)
12. Can you watch . . . ?	(the game)

11 Fill in: me you him her it us them

1. It's Helga's birthday next week. Let's buy a present for . . . . 2. Sorry, Dave. I can't come with . . . . I must take the dog for a walk. 3. Tom must be in his room. I can hear . . . . 4. I can't answer your question now. Ask . . . again tonight. 5. There must be three packets of crisps on the table. Fetch . . . , please. 6. Hallo, Mum. We're at Woodside. It's raining. Can you fetch . . . in the car? 7. Sandra and her mother are preparing the food for Sandra's party. Let's help . . . . 8. That new record is great. You must listen to . . . .

12 WORDS WORDS WORDS

a *Be careful with these three words:* **two   too   to**

1. The . . . boys are very tired. 2. We're very tired, ... 3. It's only . . . miles . . . Woodside. 4. My brother isn't . . . young. He's ten. 5. Let's go . . . the swimming-pool. 6. Is . . . o'clock OK? 7. I can hear you. Can you hear me, . . . ? 8. Listen . . . my . . . new cassettes. 9. What are you . . . doing here? 10. Jane's . . . friends are coming . . . my birthday party, ...

b *Bill is writing to his pen-friend Katrin in Bonn. But poor Bill has got problems with his pen. Can you write his letter again?*

Dear Katrin,   November 22

Th**…**k you for the letter and the magaz**…** I can re**…** your German, but I've got probl**…** with the German in "Der Tierfreund". Tha**…**s for the photo. "Langohr" is a fun**…** name for**…** rabbit. Is it "Longear" in Engli**…**? Here's a photo for you, too. It's my bir**…** party. The boy is Tim, and the girls **…** Susie and Kelly. They **…** my best fr**…**ds. I've got some great birthd**…** **…**sents. A ca**…**ette with my favourite singer from my sister, and a new bike from my grandf**…**er. The best present is from A**…** Mary. It's a hamster. It's a he. I still haven't got a name for him. Ha**…** you got an i**…**a? I must stop now and fet**…** some bisc**…**s for the hamster. He's hungry and bis**…**ts are his fa**…**rite food.

Yours,
Bill

c *Complete these sentences with "rhyme words".*

"say"-sound [eɪ]   "here"-sound [ɪə]   "my"-sound [aɪ]

1. **May**. I touch the dog?   4. The farm is ... the town.   7. ...'m German.
2. It's a nice ... today.   5. Happy birthday, ... John.   8. Birds can ... .
3. We're on our ... .   6. ... on our way.   9. ... is Peanut wet?

13 *Look at "The birthday present" on page 51 again. – Now try this:*

It is Kevin's birthday. Kevin's ... are at his ... . Liz and Sandra are there, too. They have got a ... for ... .

Liz: Happy ... , Kevin. This is for ... .
Kevin: For ... ? That's ... .
Sandra: Well, ... it.
Kevin: OK. Oh, a ... . And it's Lulu. She's my ... singer. ... , Liz and Sandra.
Liz: You're ... .

14 *Revision:* It's eleven o'clock on Saturday morning. What are our friends in Hatfield doing?

1. **Is** Kevin **repairing** (repair) his bike? No, he **isn't**. He **'s repairing** (repair) Tina's bike.
2. What ... Carol ... (do)? She's at a shop. She ... (buy) a cassette.
3. ... Mr Dean ... (help) Mrs Dean? Yes, he ... . He ... (make) some sandwiches.
4. ... Liz and Peter ... (talk) to Mr Singh? Yes, they ... . They ... (ask) him a question.
5. Where are Sally and Sandra? They're at the swimming-pool. They ... (swim) now.
6. ... Mr King ... (work) today? Yes, he ... . He ... (paint) a house.
7. What ... Tom Green ... (do)? ... he ... (do) his homework? No, he ... . He ... (watch) TV.
8. Where's Dave? He's at a record shop. He ... (buy) a record for Sandra's birthday.
9. What ... Kevin's rabbit Blacky ... (do)? Blacky ... (sit) in the garden.

15 *Sounds*

[ðə] - [ðɪ] the book, the old book, the animals, the party,   [ð] **this**, they, there, father, with
the invitation, the German boy, the English   [θ] **three**, thing, thanks, birthday, month
girl, the idea, the good idea

The birthday party is at three in the afternoon. Are there thirteen months in a year? Thanks for the nice birthday present. Their mother is 33 and their father is 35.

16 Listening comprehension: "The Black House"

Was sage ich, wenn ...	
... ich möchte, dass der Lehrer ein Wort an die Tafel schreibt?	Can you write "lively" on the board, please?
... ich die Hausaufgabe(n) noch einmal erklärt haben möchte?	Can you explain the homework again, please?
... ich auf Deutsch antworten möchte?	May I answer / say that in German, please?

1 Der bestimmte und der unbestimmte Artikel (The definite and the indefinite article)

	Vor Konsonanten:		Vor Vokalen:	
Der bestimmte Artikel:	the [ðə]	rabbit German girl party	the [ðɪ]	animal English girl invitation
Der unbestimmte Artikel:	a [ə]	young man nice uncle	an [ən]	old man uncle

2 This, that — these, those

Singular

◀ **This** is an old **house**. Dies/Das (hier) ist ein altes Haus.

That school is new. ▶  Die Schule (da) ist neu.

Plural

◀ **These rabbits** are white. Diese/Die Kaninchen (hier) sind weiß.

Those are Dad's **books**. ▶  Das (da) sind Vatis Bücher.

This und *that* (im Singular), *these* und *those* (im Plural) können oft unterschiedslos verwendet werden. Aber wenn etwas weiter entfernt ist, werden *that* (im Singular) und *those* (im Plural) verwendet.

3 Personalpronomen, Objektform (Personal pronouns, object form)

I can't do this. Can you help **me**?
You're too quiet. I can't hear **you**.
Dave? No, **he** isn't here. We can't ask **him**.
Sally? Yes, **she**'s here. We can ask **her**.
It has got a puncture, but Liz can repair **it**.
We're still at school. Can you fetch **us**?
Kevin and Dave, where are **you**? I can't hear **you**.
They're on the balcony. Carol is talking to **them**.

> ⚠ Can you help me?
> Kannst du **mir** helfen?
>
> Can you see me?
> Kannst du **mich** sehen?
>
> Englisch: *me, you, …*
> Deutsch: *mich/mir, dich/dir, …*

Die Uhrzeit angeben — **The time**

1 What time is it? Look at the clocks.

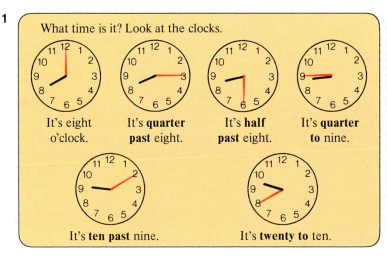

It's eight o'clock. It's **quarter past** eight. It's **half past** eight. It's **quarter to** nine.

It's **ten past** nine. It's **twenty to** ten.

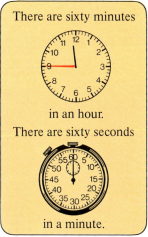

There are sixty minutes in an hour.
There are sixty seconds in a minute.

2

Kevin has got a new watch. What time is it?
It's three twenty-five.

1. It's two twenty-five.
2. It's ...
3. ... *Go on.*

3 When's the next bus? When's the next train?

It's at twenty to seven.   It's at five ...   It's ...   *Go on.*

4

1. When's the party? — It's at ...   2. When's the film? — It's ...   3. ...   *Go on.*

Unit 6 A

1 **British schools**

In Britain school is from Monday till Friday.

At some schools pupils must wear uniforms.

Lessons are in the morning and in the afternoon.

Pupils can eat lunch at school.

Pupils must do their homework in the evening.

Den Schultag beschreiben; sagen, was man regelmäßig tut

2 Park School

Dave, Kevin, Liz and Sandra **go** to Park School. Dave and Kevin go together every morning. They walk to school. Liz and Sandra go by bike.
Their lessons start at quarter past nine. Liz and Sandra eat lunch at school. Dave and Kevin go home for lunch.
In the afternoons lessons finish at four o'clock. But the pupils get homework, too. After school Dave and his friends go home or they meet at a school club.

> **And in Germany?**
>
> Pupils go to school ...
> Lessons are ...
> start at ...
> finish ...
> Pupils do their homework ...

→ Ex 1-3

3 Children at British schools have got lots of clubs. There are some interesting clubs at Park School. There's a model club. There's a ...

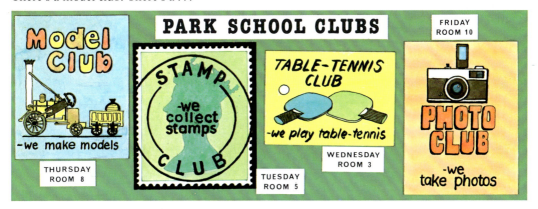

Some pupils make models. They meet every Thursday. Some pupils collect .... They meet every ...

4 Dave King, his sister Sally, and their friends at Park School are all in school clubs.

Dave King: I **make** models.
 I go to the model club.
 We **meet** in room eight every Thursday.

Kevin Connor:

Sandra Bell: I play ...
 I go to the ...
 We ...

Tom Green:

Sally King:

Liz Dean:

Über Hobbys reden

5 Hobbies

Dave King **makes** models.
He **goes** to the model club.

Tom Green collects stamps.
He goes to the stamp club.

Sandra Bell **plays** table-tennis.
She . . . .

Liz . . . table-tennis and . . . photos. She . . . .   Sally . . . models and . . . stamps. She . . . .

> **Ask a partner.**
>
> Who collects stamps? — Tom.
> Who makes models? — Dave.
> Who goes to the photo club? — . . .
> . . .

6 But they've got other hobbies, too.

Sally collects coins.
She plays football, too.

Dave plays the guitar.
He learns the piano, too.

Tom . . .   Sandra . . .

*

Kevin and Carol . . .
Liz and Peter . . .

	What's your hobby?		**And your friend's hobby?**	
I	collect . . .	Andreas	collects . . .	
	make . . .		makes . . .	
	play . . .	Petra	plays . . .	
	read . . .		reads . . .	

→ Ex 4

7 Kevin Connor takes photos. He hasn't got a camera, so he **uses** his father's old camera.

Mr Connor has got a hobby, too: tennis.
He plays it and **watches** it on TV.

Passt auf! Das "-s" nicht vergessen!

I collect stamps.		Sally She	**collects** coins.
We play table-tennis.		Simon He	**plays** football.
Kevin and Carol	take photos.	Mr Connor He	**watches** TV every evening.
They			

Sagen, was jemand regelmäßig tut und was er gerade tut; sagen, was jemand nicht tun soll

8 A teacher's day

From Monday till Friday:
Mr Hill gets up at half past six every day. He makes breakfast at seven o'clock. He eats toast and drinks a nice cup of tea or coffee. He leaves home at . . . . He arrives at school at . . . . He goes home . . . . And at the weekend? He does the housework.

> **And you?**
>
> I get up at ...
> My brother/sister gets up ...
> My father/mother gets up ...
> I leave home ...

→ S 1 · Ex 5, 6

9 Now and every day

1. It's quarter to eight. Kevin **is getting up** <u>now</u>. He **gets up** at quarter to eight <u>every day</u>.
2. It's eight o'clock. Kevin's mother is making toast now. She ... at ... every day.
3. It's ...   *Go on.*

→ S 2 · Ex 7

10 It's half past nine and Mr Hill is with class 1F. Some children aren't listening. Dave is talking to Kevin.

Mr Hill: Dave, listen to me, please.
           Don't talk to Kevin.
Dave: Sorry, sir.
Mr Hill: Where's Simon Cooper?
Sandra: He's ill, sir. He has got a cold.
Mr Hill: Thank you, Sandra. And where's Liz Dean? Has she got a cold, too?
Liz: I'm here, sir. Sorry I'm late.
Mr Hill: That's all right. But don't be late again, Liz.

→ S 3 · Ex 8-10

> **Don't** listen to Kevin. = **Do not** listen to Kevin.

6 T

New friends

Mr Hill has not got a family, but he has got two pets: a dog and a cat. The dog's name is Sebastian and the cat's name is Mozart.

Every day Mr Hill gets up at half past six and takes Sebastian for a walk. But Sebastian is very big and very lazy. They go to the park near Mr Hill's house. Every morning it is the same. Mr Hill says, "Run, Sebastian! Go, boy! Catch the ball!" But Sebastian only sits on the grass and looks at the trees. He looks at the sun and he looks at the people.

It is Saturday morning now and Mr Hill is in the park with Sebastian. It is a very nice day. Sebastian is sitting on the grass and Mr Hill says, "Go, Sebastian! Run, boy!" But Sebastian can see another dog. And the other dog can see Sebastian.

Now Sebastian is running across the grass. And Mr Hill is running after him. "Sebastian, you crazy dog. Come here!"

Now Sebastian is with his new friend, and the two dogs are playing together. Mr Hill and the other dog's owner are watching them. Mr Hill says, "OK, Sebastian. Let's go home now."

"Well," says the young woman, "I'm going home, too. We can walk together."

"Oh, that's a good idea. But listen, there's a very nice café near here. We can go there for a cup of coffee and our dogs can play."

"Yes, all right. I've got some time."

"Great. Erm . . . my name is . . ."

"Hill."

"You know my name?"

"Yes. My name is Brown. Janet Brown. My sister Pam is in your class."

"Oh, no!"

"But we can still go to the café together."

Right or wrong?

(Lines 1-6): 1. Mr Hill has got three pets. – That's wrong. Mr Hill has got two pets: a cat and a dog. 2. Mr Hill has not got a family. – That's right. 3. He gets up at half past seven and takes Mozart for a walk. 4. He takes his dog for a walk in the street. 5. Sebastian is a very lively dog.
(Lines 7-14): 6. It is Sunday now and Mr Hill is in the park with Mozart. 7. The sun is shining. 8. Sebastian is running after a cat.
(Lines 15-31): 9. The two dogs are sitting on the grass. 10. The dog's owner is a young man. 11. The young woman knows Mr Hill's name. 12. Her friend is in Mr Hill's class.

→ Ex 12

6 Ex

1 *My silly old watch is wrong again!*

1. Seven o'clock can't be the right time.
   − No, your watch is wrong. It's quarter past seven.
2. Half past three can't be the right time.
   − No, your . . . . It's . . . .
3. *Go on.*

2 *When's the next train? When's the next bus?*

LONDON	HATFIELD	DOVER	OXFORD	YORK
9.47	6.58	12.19	4.37	10.43

1. When's the next train to London, please?
   − At nine forty-seven. Thank you.
2. When's the next bus to Hatfield, please?
   − At . . . . Thank you.
3. *Go on.*

3 *Kevin and his friends*

Fill in: **do   eat   finish   go** (4×)   **help   listen to   meet   play   start   walk   watch**

1. They . . . to school from Monday till Friday.
2. Some friends . . . to school by bike, some . . . by bus, and some . . . to school.
3. Lessons . . . at quarter past nine in the morning and . . . at four o'clock in the afternoon.
4. Lots of Kevin's friends . . . lunch at school, but some . . . home for lunch.
5. Some friends . . . at a school club after school.
6. Some . . . their homework together.
7. Some . . . football or table-tennis or . . . records.
8. Some . . . their parents in the garden at the weekends.
9. Some . . . TV every evening.

4 *What are their hobbies?*

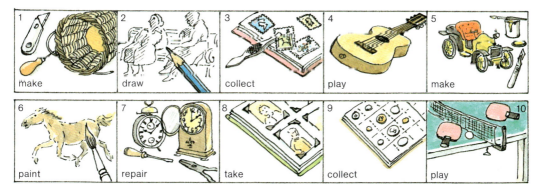

1. Sandra makes baskets. 2. Paul draws . . . . 3. Tom . . . . 4. Dave . . . . 5. Mr Green . . . .
6. Jane . . . . 7. Mr White . . . . 8. Mrs White . . . . 9. Sally . . . . 10. Liz . . . .

6 Ex

5 *What they do every day:*

Anne gets up at 6.30.
She leaves home . . . .
Go on.
Susan and Judy . . . .
Go on.

	Anne	Susan and Judy	Bill	Liz and Sandra
get up:	6.30	7.00	7.15	8.00
leave home:	8.10	8.25	8.40	8.45
go to school:	by bike	by bus	walk	by bike
in the evening:	read a book	play records	watch TV	play table-tennis

6 *My family*

*Fill in the right form ("eat**s**" or "eat"):* **eat   get up** (2×)   **go   leave   make   play   sleep   take**

"I'm Peanut the dog. I'm four months old. My home is a nice 🧺 at Liz Dean's 🏠 . I . . . in my 🧺 from **10:00** in the evening till **6:30** in the morning. Mrs Dean . . . at **6:45** every morning. I . . . at the same time. Mrs Dean . . . breakfast for the family and me. I . . . 🍪 for breakfast. After breakfast Liz . . . me for a short walk. She . . . home at **8:10** . She . . . to 🏫 by 🚲 . Liz's father is nice, too. He . . . 🎾 with me in the evenings and at the weekends."

○ **7** *Now and every day*

a 1. Sandra feeds her dog every day, but she isn't feeding him now.
   2. Jane . . . every day, but she . . . now.
   3. Dave . . . every day, but he . . . now.
   4. Mr Hill . . . every day, but . . . now.
   5. Mr King . . . in the garden every day, but . . . now.

b *And what are they all doing now?*
   1. Sandra is taking her dog for a walk.
   2. Jane . . . .
   3. Dave . . . .
      Go on.

8 *Don't do that, Kevin.*

Kevin

Sally

Tom

Dave

Peanut

1. Don't climb . . . , Kevin.   2. . . . Dave's . . . , Sally.   3. . . . Clare's . . . , Tom.   *Go on.*

9 In English, please.

Was kannst du sagen,

1. wenn Peter sich nicht so dumm anstellen soll? — Don't be silly, Peter.
2. wenn Dave den Hund nicht anfassen soll? — Don't touch . . . .
3. wenn Kate nicht zu spät kommen soll? — Don't . . . .
4. wenn Kevin nicht auf seine Schwestern hören soll? — . . .
5. wenn Liz das nicht noch mal sagen soll? — . . .
6. wenn Dave nicht alle Kuchen essen soll? — . . .
7. wenn Kevin nicht auf Dave warten soll? — . . .
8. wenn Sally nicht noch mal diese Cassette spielen soll? — . . .
9. wenn Carol das nicht noch mal machen soll? — . . .

10 Say it in English: *sich bei jemandem bedanken*

Meist bedankt man sich im Englischen mit	**Thank you.** **Thanks.**
Im Englischen reagiert man darauf nie mit "please", sondern mit einem dieser Ausdrücke	**That's all right.** **That's OK.** **You're welcome.**

Work with a partner. It's Kevin's birthday. Look at his presents.

1. *Kevin:* Thank you for the camera, Dad. It's great.
   Mr Connor: That's all right.
2. *Kevin:* Thanks for . . . . It's fantastic.
   Carol: You're . . . .

   Go on.

11 WORDS WORDS WORDS

a *One, two, three. Find the third word.*

1. spring, summer, *autumn*
2. January, February, . . .
3. June, August, . . .
4. Friday, Saturday, . . .
5. week, month, . . .
6. morning, afternoon, . . .
7. first, second, . . .
8. fifteen, thirty, . . .
9. quarter past, half past, . . .
10. a second, a minute, . . .

b *Odd man out!*

In jeder Reihe steht ein Wort, das nicht zu den übrigen passt. Welches?

1. hamster bird mouse dog
2. nice fantastic great lazy
3. box bottle bag basket
4. café tea juice lemonade
5. train bike bus car
6. English British French Germany
7. uncle aunt brother father man
8. come go sleep leave walk

6 Ex

c sing → song   A new letter → a new word
   pet → pe**n**

   bark → ...   1. Jane is waiting for us in the ... .
   same → ...   2. What's your new teacher's ... ?
   catch → ...   3. There's a great football ... on TV tonight.
   big → ...   4. Can't the magazine be in your ... ?
   make → ...   5. Please, can you ... the dog for a walk?
   can → ...   6. Let's feed the ... .
   some → ...   7. The two pupils are from the ... village.
   on → ...   8. I can't read this letter. It's ... Japanese.

d *Find the missing words.*

   1. (auf) ... the table   7. (im) ... the garden   13. talk (mit) ... Mr White
   2. (am) ... Friday   8. (in) ... Germany   14. wait (auf) ... the next bus
   3. (am) ... the evening   9. (im) ... the radio   15. walk (über) ... the street
   4. (am) ... the weekend   10. (aus) ... Dover   16. play (mit) ... his parents
   5. (auf) ... the street   11. (um) ... five o'clock   17. go (mit) ... bike
   6. (auf) ... German   12. (nach) ... school   18. go (in) ... school

e *Fill in:* **at** (3×) **for** (2×) **from** (2×) **on** (3×) **till** **to** (2×) **with**

   1. The exercise is ... page 54. 2. Jane is still ... school. 3. She goes ... school ... nine ... four. 4. Kevin goes home ... lunch and Liz eats lunch ... school. 5. Let's meet Jane ... the school club. 6. Who is that ... the phone? 7. You can listen ... this programme again ... Saturday. 8. Those cassettes are a present ... Tina ... her grandmother. 9. Who can help me ... the housework?

12 *Look at "New friends" on page 62 again. Now look at the words and pictures.*

Susan Jones — dog. name — Toby. **Every day** — come home — school — half past four — take — Toby — walk. Toby — small — lively. go — park — near — house. Every afternoon — play — same game. Susan — say — run — go — catch — ball. Toby — run — across — grass — to — trees — fetch — ball.

Now — Friday afternoon — Susan — park — Toby. But — can see — another dog.

Toby — run after — him.

Now — play — together.

Now — Susan — other dog's owner — sit — grass. They — drink — lemonade — talk.

Now write some sentences. You can start:
Susan Jones has got a dog. His name is Toby. Every day Susan comes home from school at ...

13 Revision: *short forms – long forms*

1. You're my best friend, Karen. You are my best friend, Karen.
2. John isn't ten, he's eleven. John is not . . . .
3. We're writing sentences. . . .
4. Where's Petra? . . .
5. I've got a pen, I haven't got a pencil. . . .
6. There's a new girl in our class. . . .
7. Clare can't come to my party. . . .
8. Bob hasn't got his French book. . . .

14 Revision: *German* **"IHR"** → *English* **her   their   you   your**

1. What are . . . two doing? — We're waiting for Clare. 2. Is that . . . cat, Miss Doyle? — Yes, . . . name is Lizzy. 3. Look, there are Jane and . . . parents. — Is that VW . . . car? 4. Yes, Carol is in . . . room. — Can we talk to . . . , please? 5. This is Kevin and Carol and . . . sister Tina.

15

[ɔː]	**a**ll, t**a**ll, t**a**lk, **Au**gust, m**or**ning	[uː] **foo**d, s**oo**n, J**u**ne, y**ou**, d**o**, wh**o**
[ɒ]	**To**m, d**o**g, w**a**tch, wh**a**t, **o**range, **a**cross	[ʊ] **goo**d, b**oo**k, l**oo**k, f**oo**tball, w**o**man
[ɔɪ]	b**oy**, t**oi**let	[j] **y**es, **y**ou, **u**niform, n**e**w, p**u**pil

Tom is a tall boy. Bob's new hobby is football. All the boys are talking. Look at this good book. A new café with good food. Who is looking at the woman in uniform?

Was sage ich, wenn . . .							
. . . ich die	Hefte / Bücher	verteilen möchte?		Can I give out the	exercise books, / books,		please?
. . . ich das Fenster		öffnen / schließen	möchte?	Can I	open / shut	the window, please?	
. . . ich	den nächsten Satz / Daves Rolle	lesen möchte?		May I read	the next sentence, / Dave's part,		please?

The fifteen-second game

Suche in Zeitschriften, Katalogen usw. Fotos von 15 Gegenständen, deren englische Namen dir bekannt sind. Klebe die Fotos auf ein Blatt Papier.

An interesting job?

The pupils in class 1F must write a report about people with interesting jobs. Sandra Bell's report is about a disc jockey on the radio. She thinks it is a fantastic job.

> Dear Dave Sales,
> We must make a report for our English teacher about people with interesting jobs. I think you've got a fantastic job. You can play all your favourite records. You meet lots of pop stars. Can you please tell me about your job?
> Yours,
> Sandra Bell
> PS You're my favourite DJ!!

> Dear Sandra,
> Thanks for your letter. Why not come to the studio next week? We can talk about my job here.
> But I can tell you now: a DJ's job isn't so very interesting.
> Yours,
> Dave Sales

This is Sandra's report:
Dave Sales is a disc jockey. He works for City Radio. His programme starts at seven o'clock, so he must get up at quarter past five every morning. That is not very nice.

He makes toast and a cup of tea. He cannot read the newspaper because it comes at eight o'clock.

The programme starts at seven o'clock. There are no pop stars on his programme — not at seven o'clock in the morning!

He plays records till eight o'clock. At eight o'clock it is time for the news — and for a cup of tea and some biscuits. The tea is not very nice at City Radio!

At quarter past eight Dave starts work again. He makes lots of jokes on his programme. They are terrible!

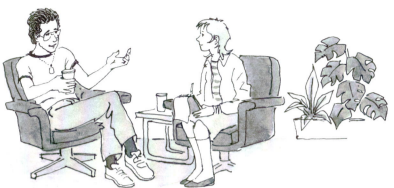

Sandra is at the studio with Dave Sales. She is talking to him about his job.

He leaves home at quarter to six, and goes to London in his car.

He listens to his car radio every morning — City Radio, of course!

He arrives at quarter to seven. His records for the programme are in a box. He cannot play his favourite records.

Dave finishes work at half past ten from Monday till Friday. On Saturday he has got a programme in the afternoon.

He goes home in his car, takes the dog for a walk, reads the newspaper . . . and plays records.

A disc jockey's job is not very interesting!

69

1 Die einfache Form des Präsens (The simple present)

a  Aber:

Das *simple present* hat für alle Personen (mit Ausnahme der 3. Person Singular) dieselbe Form wie der Infinitiv.

⚠ Die 3. Person Singular endet als einzige Form immer auf *-s*.

b **Die 3. Person Singular** (The third person singular)

[-z]	[-s]	[-ɪz]
play**s**	help**s**	use**s**
read**s**	eat**s**	finish**es**
leave**s**	take**s**	watch**es**
wear**s**	laugh**s**	fetch**es**

Für die Aussprache des *-s* der 3. Person Singular gelten die gleichen Regeln wie für das Plural-*s* (siehe Seite 46).

Passt auf bei der Schreibung und Aussprache dieser Formen:

I finish — he/she finish**es**	I hurr**y** — he/she hurr**ies**	I s**ay** — he/she s**ays** [sez]
I watch — he/she watch**es**	I carr**y** — he/she carr**ies**	I go — he/she go**es** [gəʊz]
I fetch — he/she fetch**es**	I pla**y** — he/she pla**ys**	I do — he/she do**es** [dʌz]

c **Gebrauch**

Dave and Kevin **walk** to school every morning.
Dave und Kevin gehen jeden Morgen zu Fuß zur Schule.

Sandra **plays** table-tennis every week.
Sandra spielt jede Woche Tischtennis.

They **go** home for lunch.
Sie gehen zum Mittagessen nach Hause.

She **collects** stamps, too.
Sie sammelt auch Briefmarken.

Wir verwenden das *simple present*, wenn jemand etwas regelmäßig, z.B. auch als Hobby, tut.

○ 2 The simple present and the present progressive⁺

Den deutschen Satz „Sally spielt Fußball" muss man im Englischen — je nachdem, was man ausdrücken will — durch zwei verschiedene Sätze wiedergeben:
1. Sally **plays** football (every week). Das heißt, sie spielt regelmäßig Fußball.
2. Sally **is playing** football (now). Das heißt, sie spielt jetzt/gerade.

Wenn jemand jetzt/gerade etwas tut, so verwenden wir das *present progressive*.

3 Der verneinte Imperativ (The negative imperative)

	Be quiet. (Sei/Seid ruhig!)
Don't	be silly. (Sei/Seid nicht albern!)
Don't	do that, please, Kevin.
Don't	feed Peanut now, please, Liz and Peter.

Der Imperativ wird verneint durch das Voranstellen der Kurzform *don't* [dəʊnt].
Don't wird sowohl für den Singular als auch für den Plural verwendet.

⁺ Auf die Unterschiede zwischen den beiden Formen wird in den Units 7 und 8 ausführlicher eingegangen.

Das Haus oder die Wohnung beschreiben **Unit 7 A**

Merlin the Magician

1 This is Merlin the Magician:

and this is his rabbit, Dr K. Nickel:

They live together in a *very* funny house. All the rooms of the house are a different colour and they're in funny places.

2 Downstairs there's a green room with lots of books about magic. This is Merlin's library. The desk and the shelves are green, too. The library is the room where Merlin does his magic. Next to the library is the living-room. Here Merlin reads the paper or watches TV. Everything is brown in this room: the walls, the floor and the ceiling. The library is between the living-room and the small blue bedroom. Merlin's rabbit, Dr K. Nickel, sleeps in this bedroom.

3 Upstairs there's a grey kitchen where Merlin and Dr K. Nickel cook their meals. The kitchen is over the living-room and under the dining-room. In the dining-room everything is orange: the chairs, the table and the cupboard. Over the dining-room is the red bathroom and Merlin's yellow bedroom. Of course, his bed and his lamp are yellow, too.

Inside the house, there are stairs, and outside there's a ladder. Isn't it a funny house?

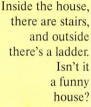

4 Where's Merlin's bedroom? — It's over ...
　　　　　　 living-room? — It's under ...
　　　　　　　　 ... ? — It's next to ...
What colour is the ... ? — It's red/blue/...

Ask a partner.

Where's your room? — It's next to/over ...
　　　　　　　　　 — I haven't got a room.
　　　　　　　　　 — I share my room with ...
Have you got a ... in your room?
What colour is your ... ?

7A

Sagen, wie oft jemand etwas tut

5 Merlin hasn't got a job. But he's lucky. He can do magic. And Dr K. Nickel works for him, too. He paints his rooms for him every week.
Mr King can't do magic. He must go to work. He paints houses. He works from Monday till Friday.
He gets up at seven o'clock and **always** leaves the house at eight o'clock.
He **usually** comes home at six o'clock, but he **sometimes** comes home later.
He **often** watches football on Saturday afternoon, but not every week.
He **never** works on Sunday, of course.

6

I sometimes …	… go to school on Saturday.	… play football/table-tennis.
I often …	… read comics.	… arrive home at …
I usually …	… go to the swimming-pool.	… get up at …
I never …	… walk to school.	… eat lunch at home.
I always …	… watch TV in the evenings.	… go to school by bike.
	… help my parents in the kitchen.	

→ S 1 · Ex 1, 2

7

It's Saturday morning.
Dave is helping his father **now**.
They're painting a room.
Dave **often helps** his father on Saturday morning.

Sally sometimes helps her father, too.
But she isn't helping him at the moment. She's playing football.

8

1. Mrs King is taking the dog for a walk.
   She sometimes takes the dog for a walk in the evening.
2. Sally is … football with her friends.
   She always … football on Saturdays.
3. Dave … to school.
   He …
4. Mr King …
   He …
5. It's eight o'clock. Merlin …
   But he … at eight o'clock on Sunday morning, of course.

→ S 2 · Ex 3

Über die Arbeit im Hause sprechen

7A

9 Jobs at home

There are lots of jobs in every home. You must ...

... cook the meals.

... wash the dishes. ... dry the dishes.

... make the beds. ... tidy up the rooms.

And in your family?

I usually make ...
My mother always ...
My father sometimes ...
My brother/sister never ...
I often ...

10

Some mothers **go** to work.
Some mothers **don't go** to work.
They stay at home
and do the housework.

Mrs King and Mrs Connor stay at home,
but I **don't stay** at home.
I work in an office in Hatfield.
I eat with my family in the morning,
but we **don't eat** together in the
evening. My husband is a mechanic
and he sometimes comes home late.
We do the housework together when
we come home.

Mrs Dean

Mrs King

→ Ex 4

11

I think my family is terrible.
Sally tidies up her room,
but Dave **doesn't tidy up** his room.
My husband often cooks the meals,
but he doesn't tidy up the kitchen.
Sally washes the dishes,
but she doesn't dry them.
I always tidy up after them.

And in your family?

My mother/father	stays ...
	doesn't stay ...
My sister/brother	tidies up ...
	doesn't tidy up ...
We	eat ...	in the morning/evening.
	don't eat ...
I	wash and dry ...
	don't wash and dry ...

→ S 3 · Ex 5, 6

I **don't** play football. = I **do not** play football.
Liz **doesn't** play tennis. = Liz **does not** play tennis.

7 T

The new rooms

The Connors live in a flat in Hatfield. It is a big flat with three bedrooms. Mr Connor and his wife have got the small bedroom. Kevin has got the second bedroom. His sisters, Tina and Carol, must share the third bedroom. And that is the problem. The two girls argue day and night. They argue because Carol's desk is under the window and Tina's desk is between the cupboard and the door.
5 They argue because the record-player is behind Carol's bed, but the records are on a shelf over Tina's 5
bed. They argue about the colour of the chairs, the cupboards and the other furniture. They argue about everything.

Today Mr Connor is making a wall through their room. He is making two small rooms.

10 Mr Connor: OK. You've got a wall between you now. So don't argue.
Carol: Can we paint the rooms?
Mr Connor: You can paint everything: the walls, the ceiling, the cupboards. But
15 please don't argue!

The two sisters are painting their rooms and their furniture now. Carol likes brown, yellow and white, but Tina does not like these colours. She likes green, blue, red and orange.

Carol: Your orange cupboard is all right, but green chairs! That's a terrible combination!
Tina: I don't think so. And I don't like your room. 20
Who likes yellow walls? I think they're terrible.
Carol: Sorry, but I don't agree. *I* don't like your green chairs with your orange cupboard.
Tina: Well, stay in your room and don't come in my room. 25
Carol: OK, but you can't have my records.
Tina: Good. I don't like your silly old records.

Mr Connor is in the room now.

Mr Connor: Tina! Carol! Be quiet. Now listen to me. Don't argue. Or you can have a new room — in the 30
garage!

Correct these sentences:

(Lines 1-7): 1. The Connors live in a small flat. – No. The Connors don't live in a small flat. They live in a big flat. 2. Kevin and Carol share a bedroom. 3. Tina and Kevin argue day and night.
(Lines 8-15): 4. Mr Connor is making a wall through the living-room. 5. The girls can paint everything in the flat.
(Lines 16-31): 6. The two girls like the same colours. 7. Carol likes the colour of Tina's chairs. 8. Tina likes the colour of Carol's walls. 9. Tina likes Carol's records. 10. Mr Connor says they can have a new room downstairs.
→ Ex 8, 9

7 Ex

1 *Find the right places for these words:*

always   never   often   sometimes   usually

1. Mr Singh works at his pet shop from Monday till Friday. And he works on Saturdays, too. (always, sometimes)
Mr Singh always works at his pet shop from Monday till Friday. And he sometimes works on Saturdays, too.
2. He comes home from work at six in the evening. But he comes home for lunch, too. (usually, often)
3. In the evening he reads a book or a magazine. He reads comics. (sometimes, never)
4. Mrs Singh watches TV in the evening. But at the weekend she reads a book or listens to records. (usually, sometimes)
5. Her favourite pet is her cat Tiger. She buys the best things for Tiger. (always)
6. Mr Singh's favourite pet is his dog Prince. He waits for Mr Singh in the evenings. In the mornings Prince runs after Mr Singh's car. (usually, always)

2 *Be careful with the word order.*

1. Tom/comes/often/from school at five o'clock/home.
Tom often comes home from school at five o'clock.
2. Tom's sister/with his homework/sometimes/helps him.
3. His sister/goes to guitar lessons/always/on Mondays.
4. Her dog/waits for her/always/in the garden.
5. She/cleans/on Saturdays/usually/the dog's basket.
6. Her mother/at a pet shop/usually/the food for the dog/buys.

3 *Look at the pictures and complete the sentences.*

1. Carol ..**is taking**.. a photo of her parents. She often .**takes**. photos of other people, too.
2. Sally's mother usually ... the breakfast. But today she has got a cold, so Sally ... the breakfast.
3. Tom often ... football with Sally. Today he ... with Dave and Kevin.
4. Mr Singh ... in his pet shop. It's Sunday today and he ... in the garden.
5. Dr K. Nickel's hobby is magic. He can't do magic today. He ... his room.
6. Sandra ... a model of a car. She sometimes ... models of other things, too.
7. Liz ... a comic. She ... books about interesting people, too.
8. Jane ... pictures of animals. Today she ... a picture of a budgie.

7 Ex

4 *"That's wrong." — Correct the sentences.*

1. The Connors come from Oxford. — That's wrong. The Connors don't come from Oxford. They come from Dover. 2. The Kings live near Hatfield. — That's wrong. The Kings don't . . . . They live . . . Hatfield. 3. Kevin and Dave go to different schools. 4. In Britain pupils wear uniforms at *all* schools. 5. In Britain pupils do their homework in the morning. 6. Lessons at Park School start at half past ten. 7. Lessons at Park School finish after lunch. 8. Liz and Sandra walk to school.

5 *Look at the pictures and say what the people do and what they don't do.*

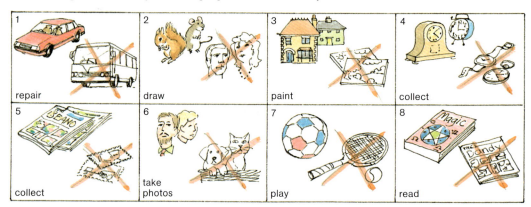

1. Mr Dean repairs cars.   2. Jane draws . . . .   3. Mr King . . .   4. Mr Singh . . .
   He doesn't repair buses.   She doesn't . . . .   He . . . .
5. Liz . . .   6. Mrs Singh . . .   7. Dave . . .   8. Merlin . . .

6 *Fill in:* **don't – doesn't**

1. Where's Sandra?
   — I . . . know.
2. Sally plays the guitar.
   — No, she . . . . Her brother plays the guitar.
3. Is this Kevin's bike?
   — We . . . know.
4. Is this your magazine?
   — Oh no. I . . . read magazines for girls.
5. I read lots of comics but my sister . . . read comics.
6. Where's Susan?
   — She's at home. She . . . go to football matches.
7. I think Mr Singh plays tennis.
   — No, he . . . .
8. Have the Whites got a camera?
   — Yes, but they don't often take photos.

7 WORDS WORDS WORDS

a **What? When? Where? Who?**

Fill in the right question word.

1. . . . can answer this question?
2. . . .'s the toilet, please?
3. . . . can carry this box upstairs?
4. . . . are the letters?
5. . . .'s the next French lesson? Today?
6. . . . feeds your rabbit?
7. . . .'s in this box in the kitchen?
8. . . .'s my watch?
9. . . .'s that under the table?
10. . . .'s for homework?
11. . . . can we meet you again? Is Monday OK?
12. . . . watches TV every evening?

b *Find the partners.*

aunt boys breakfast cats chair children coffee day evening friend girls husband juice lemonade lunch men mice morning night parents partner Saturday summer Sunday table tea today tomorrow uncle wife winter women

PEOPLE (6×)
aunt and uncle
boys and ...

TIME (5×)
day and night
evening and ...

MEALS (1×)
...

ANIMALS (1×)
...

DRINKS (2×)
...

FURNITURE (1×)
...

c *Find the right word and complete the sentences.*

café
cake
calendar
camera
date
late
later
make
page
parents
same

1. This exercise is on ... 77.
2. Why not take some photos with your new ... ?
3. My father is still at work. Can you come again ... ?
4. Can't we meet at the ... near the park?
5. What ... is it next Sunday? May 15th?
6. This is my sister and these are my ... .
7. We're very hungry. Can you ... some sandwiches?
8. You don't know the date? Look at the ... .
9. Let's buy some ... for this afternoon.
10. Kevin and Dave go to the ... school.
11. Jane doesn't wear a watch. She's always ... , of course.

8 *Say it in English: sagen, was man mag oder nicht mag*

Wenn du etwas magst oder gern hast, sagst du	▶ **I like** comics.
Wenn du etwas nicht magst, sagst du	▶ **I don't like** silly TV programmes.
Und wenn du etwas wirklich gar nicht magst, sagst du	▶ **I hate** quiz programmes.

Here you can see what Dave and his friends like or don't like.

	football	table-tennis	model cars	school meals	homework	school uniforms
likes	Dave	Liz		Carol	Sandra	Carol
doesn't like	Sandra	Kevin	Sally	Kevin	Dave	Sandra
hates			Liz	Sally	Kevin	Dave

a Dave: I like football. I don't like homework. And I hate school uniforms.
Sandra: I don't like ... . I like ... . And I don't ... .
Liz: I ... .   Go on.

b Dave likes football. He doesn't like homework. And he hates school uniforms.
Sandra doesn't like ... . She likes ... . And she doesn't like ... . Liz ... .   Go on.

c *And you? And your friend(s)?*

7 Ex

9 *Look at "The new rooms" on page 74 again. Now try this:*

Carol and Tina are playing records in Carol's room.

Carol: Mike Walker is all . . . . But Jimmy White! He's a . . . singer!
Tina: Well, *I* don't . . . so. I . . . him. But who . . . Andy Black? . . . silly.
Carol: . . . , but I don't . . . . I think he's . . . .
Tina: Oh, no! He must be over 40 years . . . . And he . . . sing.
Carol: Well, . . . in your room and don't . . . in my room. You can . . . to your . . . old records there!

10 Revision: **this, these, that** *or* **those**? — *Only one of the words in ( ) is right.*

1. I can't answer (that/those) questions. 2. Can you help me with (this/these) homework? 3. Are (this/these) your records, Jane? 4. Who are (this/these) people? 5. I like (that/those) photos. 6. (That/Those) men are mechanics. 7. Are (that/those) cassettes a birthday present from your uncle? 8. Can (this/these) poster be Dave's? 9. Is (that/those) your sister's bike? 10. (This/These) are my friends Kevin and Bill.

11 Revision: *Find the plural for these words. — Be careful. Two of the words have got no plural form.*

mouse — *mice*.   child — . . .   furniture — . . .   hobby — . . .   boy — . . .   woman — . . .
match — . . .   family — . . .   homework — . . .   party — . . .   man — . . .   shelf — . . .

Now complete these sentences.

1. The Millers have got three . . . , one girl and two . . . . 2. Can dogs catch . . . , too? 3. Sally collects old coins. What are her other . . . ? 4. These . . . are a good place for your books. 5. There are two . . . in the photo: the Kings and the Walkers. 6. Liz is helping Peter with his . . . . 7. On Wednesday evenings there are often interesting football . . . on TV. 8. I like Tom's birthday . . . . There are usually lots of nice people. 9. Those two . . . are Liz's mother and her grandmother. 10. Let's paint that old . . . in different colours.

12 Revision: **What? When? Where? Who? How? Why?**

1. . . .'s your favourite colour?
   — Red.
2. . . . is that on the phone?
   — My guitar teacher.
3. . . .'s your next guitar lesson?
   — On Wednesday.
4. . . . can't you come with us?
   — Because I must finish this letter.
5. . . .'s the swimming-pool?
   — In Potters Park.
6. . . . is your best friend?
   — Wag.
7. . . . are you from?
   — Hamburg.
8. . . . are you late?
   — My watch is wrong.
9. . . .'s in the shop window?
   — Two young dogs and fifteen white mice.
10. . . . are the biscuits?
    — Great.

13 Sounds

- [ɜː] **g**i**r**l, b**ir**d, f**ir**st, w**or**k, t**ur**n, Th**ur**sday, f**ur**niture, M**er**lin, l**ear**n
- [ə] **a**gain, **a**bout, **a**gree, moth**er**, sist**er**, **a**fternoon, wom**a**n, probl**e**m, **a**t home, lots **o**f people, ten t**o** four, boys **a**nd girls, s**o**me nice pets. He m**u**st go. She c**a**n sing.
- [ɪə] **h**ere, h**ear**, n**ear**, d**ear**, **i**dea, we'**re**
- [eə] **wh**ere, w**ear**, th**ere**, th**eir**, rep**air**, ch**air**, st**air**s, sh**are**, M**ary**
- [ʊə] **p**oo**r**, yo**u're**

Merlin's furniture is lots of different colours. Her sister works at home on Thursday afternoons. Let's share the sandwiches. That's a good idea. Is there a repair shop near here? Where's the poor bird? You're a lucky girl, Mary.

14 Listening comprehension: A good cook

Was sage ich, wenn ...	
... ich etwas nicht weiß?	I'm sorry, I don't know.
... ich etwas nicht begreife?	I'm sorry, I don't understand.
... jemand lauter sprechen soll?	Can you speak louder, please?

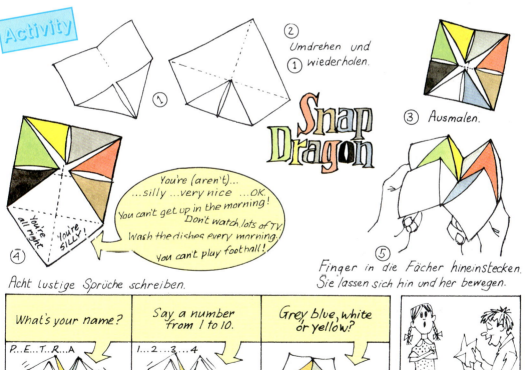

7S

1 Wortstellung (Word order)

a

Subject	Verb	Object
Kevin	is feeding	the rabbit.
Sally and Tom	play	football.
You and I	can speak	English.
The children	have got	lots of different hobbies.

Anders als im Deutschen steht das Subjekt eines englischen Aussagesatzes immer vor dem Prädikat, das Objekt nach dem Prädikat. Vergleiche:

Deutsch entweder: Carol füttert die Vögel. Kevin füttert das Kaninchen.
Oder: Die Vögel füttert Carol. Das Kaninchen füttert Kevin.

Englisch nur:	Carol	is feeding	the birds.	Kevin	is feeding	the rabbit.
	Subject	**V**erb	**O**bject	**S**ubject	**V**erb	**O**bject

⚠ Beachte die **S**traßen-**V**erkehrs-**O**rdnung, damit es keine Unfälle gibt!

b

Subject		Verb	Object	
Sandra Bell	**always**	eats	toast	for breakfast.
Kevin and Carol	**often**	do	their homework	together.
Mr King	**usually**	watches	football	on Saturday afternoons.
Sally and Dave	**sometimes**	help	their father	at the weekend.
Mr Hill	**never**	drinks	coffee	in the evening.

Wörter wie *always, often* usw. dürfen im Englischen nicht zwischen Prädikat und Objekt stehen.
Vergleiche: Sandra always eats toast. → Sandra isst immer Toast.

2 The simple present and the present progressive+

Sally can cook.
She **sometimes cooks**
the meals.

Sally **isn't cooking** a meal
at the moment.
She**'s reading** a book.

Simple present: regelmäßig, gewöhnlich, wie oft

Present progressive: im Augenblick, gerade, jetzt

3 The simple present in negative sentences

I					Dave/He		
You		**don't live** in London.		Aber:	Sally/She		**doesn't live** in London.
We					The rabbit/It		
You							
They							

Tim and Terry live in Hatfield.   Sandra live**s** in Woodside.
They **don't live** in London.   Liz doe**sn't live** in Woodside.

Kurzform: *don't*   Langform: *do not*   Kurzform: *doesn't*   Langform: *does not*

+Die Gegenüberstellung *simple present/present progressive* wird in Unit 8 noch ausführlicher dargestellt.

Über Geld und Preise reden

British money

There are a hundred pence ("p") in a pound.

45p	You say:	forty-five pence
	or:	forty-five p [piː]
£1		a pound/one pound
£1.25		one (pound) twenty-five
£2		two pounds
£5.80		five (pounds) eighty

German money

DM 0.50	You say:	fifty pfennigs
DM 1.00		a mark/one mark
DM 1.25		one (mark) twenty-five
DM 2.00		two marks
DM 3.40		three (marks) forty

Say: £89.30 27p £10
     10p   £1.50 13p
     £3.65 2p   £88.88

Say: DM 1.35 DM 0.83 DM 26.80
     DM 4.98 DM 0.49 DM 2.50
     DM 99.99 DM 0.68 DM 1.75

How much is the book? — It's ...
How much are the records? — They're ...
Go on.

The book is 95p. — Oh, that's cheap.
The ... are ...   — Oh, that's ...
...

Unit 8 A

Über Taschengeld sprechen

1 Some children **get** pocket-money every week.

Do Kevin and Dave **get** pocket-money?
— **Yes, they do.**
Do Sandra and Tom get pocket-money?
— **No, they don't.**

2 Liz: **Do you get** pocket-money every week?
Sally: **Yes, I do.** I get £2.
Tom: **No, I don't.** I ask my parents for money.
Kevin: Yes, I do. I get ...
Sandra: No, ...
... → Ex 1

3 Liz: I save 25p. **How much do you save?**
Kevin: I save 50p.
Sally: I save nothing.
Dave: ...
...

Name	Do they get pocket-money?	How much do they get?	How much do they save?
Kevin Connor	✓	£2.50	50p
Carol Connor	✓	£2.80	80p
Tina Connor	✓	£1.80	50p
Sandra Bell	✗	—	—
Sally King	✓	£2.00	—
Dave King	✓	£1.50	40p
Liz Dean	✓	£2.00	25p
Peter Dean	✓	75p	25p
Tom Green	✗	—	—

And you?

Do you get pocket-money? — Yes, I do.
　　　　　　　　　　　　　　No, I don't.
How much do you get?　　— I get ... marks a week/month.
How much do you save? — I save ... marks a week/month.

4 What do children buy with their pocket-money? Some children buy sweets; some children buy comics and magazines. Some buy pencils, books and other things.

What do Kevin and Dave buy? — Sweets.
What do ...
...

And you?

What do you buy with your pocket-money?

→ Ex 2

Kevin and Dave

Carol and Liz

Dave and Liz

Sally and Carol

Nach Gewohnheiten fragen

5 Interviews

What do you do in your free time?

Do you ...?

Where do you ...?

What do you ...?

When do you ...?

How often do you ...?

TV — Sandra Bell
How often do you watch TV? — Every day.
How long do you watch? — About two hours.
Do you like "Tom and Jerry"? — Yes, I do.

PETS — Sally King
What pets ... like? — Dogs.
Have you got a ...? — Yes, I have.
How often ... take it for a walk? — Every day.
... you clean it, too? — No, I don't.

HOBBIES — Tom Green
Have you got a hobby? — Yes, I collect stamps.
... you go to a club? — Yes, I do.
How often ... go? — Every Thursday.
What stamps ... collect? — British stamps.

SPORTS — Kevin Connor
... you like sports? — Yes, I do.
... play table-tennis? — No, I don't.
... play football? — Yes, I do.
When ... practise? — At the weekend.

→ Ex 4

Activity

Programmes

Have you got a cassette-recorder?
You can make a programme.

Good evening. Here's Hobby Magazine. Heike Braun is with us today. Heike, can I ask you about ...?

Free time
Hobbies
Sports
School
Jobs
Magazines
Money
Clubs   Music   TV   Pets

What/Where/When/How often do you ...?

Have you got ...?

Can you ...?

Do you ...?

Aussage: You watch TV every evening.   They buy sweets.
Frage: **Do** you watch TV every evening? **What do** they buy?

6 What do Sandra and her friends do **when they've got no school**?

Sandra likes hockey.
She plays hockey at Woodside Sports Club.
She practises every Wednesday.
She starts at six o'clock and finishes at eight o'clock.
→ S 1a

Woodside Sports Club
Wednesday, 6-8

7 What does Kevin like? — Football.
Where does he play? — At Sandfield Youth Club.
How often does he practise? — Every Monday.
When does he start? — At five o'clock.
When does he finish? — At half past six.

Sandfield Youth Club
monday, 5-6.30

What does Liz like? — Table-tennis.
Where ... play? — At Park School.
How often ...? — Every Wednesday.
When ...? — At four o'clock.
...? — At half past five.

Park School Table-tennis Club
Wednesday, 4-5.30

Dave likes music.
What does he play? — The guitar.
...? — ...
→ Ex 5

"I practise with a friend every Friday evening. We play from 6 till 8 o'clock."

8

Does	Liz Kevin Sandra Dave	like play practise start finish	football? table-tennis? at Woodside Youth Club? at Park School? every Monday? at 4 o'clock? the guitar? ...?	— Yes, he/she does. — Yes, of course. — No, he/she doesn't. — No, of course not.

Aussage: Sally play⬜s⬜ football.
Frage: Doe⬜s⬜ Sally play hockey, too?
Aussage: Tom collect⬜s⬜ stamps.
Frage: What doe⬜s⬜ Dave collect?

Ask a partner.
You can use these questions:
Do you play football/table-tennis/the guitar/...?
Where do you play?
How often do you practise?
When ... start/finish?

Does your brother/sister/friend play ..., too?
What does he/she play?
How often does he/she ...?

→ S 1b, 2 · Ex 3

Sagen, was jemand regelmäßig oder gerade tut

9 Kevin usually **plays** football on Saturday afternoons. He plays for Sandfield Youth Club. He often plays in Hatfield, but he sometimes plays in other towns near Hatfield.

Ask a partner.

| Do you play | football?
tennis?
hockey?
the guitar? | – Yes, I do.
– No, I don't. |

| Are you playing | football now?
tennis?
hockey?
the guitar? |

– Of course not! I'm | learning English.
talking to you.
sitting in room . . .

→ S 3 · Ex 6-8

It's Saturday afternoon now. Kevin **isn't playing** football. There isn't a match today. What's he doing? He's going to the sports shop.

10 Kevin is in the sports shop now. Liz is there, too.

Liz: Hallo, Kevin. Why aren't you playing football?
Kevin: Because there's no match today.

Assistant: Good afternoon. Can I help you?
Liz: Yes, please. Do you sell yellow tennis balls?
Assistant: Yes, here you are. There are four in a tin.
Liz: How much are they?
Assistant: £4.50. Anything else?
Liz: No, thank you.
Assistant: And what can I do for you, young man?
Kevin: Oh, I'm just looking, thank you. → Ex 9

8 T

The record-player

Liz is in the living-room with her father. It is Friday evening and Mr Dean is reading the newspaper. Liz is sitting on the sofa next to him. She has got a question.

"Dad."
"What is it? You can see that I'm reading."
"Can I have a new record-player, Dad?"
"You've got a record-player."
"Oh, that old thing. It's terrible. And it's broken."
"Can't you buy a record-player with your pocket-money? You get £2 a week. How much do you save? Or do you spend everything?"
"I save 25p a week. But a new record-player is £60 and I've only got £20."
"Well, let's look in the newspaper. People sometimes sell record-players there and they aren't expensive... Look, here's a record-player."

Liz is on the phone now.

RECORD-PLAYER stereo
Tel. 64203

"64203. Mrs Carter here."
"Hallo. I'm phoning about your record-player."
"Oh, yes. It's very nice. It's stereo."
"How much is it?"
"£22."
"Can my father and I come and look at it?"
"Yes, of course. When can you come?"
"This evening?"
"Yes, all right."
"Where do you live?"
"42 Mill Road. Goodbye."
"Bye."

Liz is talking to her father now.

"It's £22, Dad."
"Where's the problem?"
"I've only got £20. Can you give me £2, Dad?"
"No, but I can give you your pocket-money for next week now."
"And next week?"
"You can stay at home and listen to your records."

(Lines 1-16): 1. What are Liz and her father doing? 2. How much pocket-money does Liz get? 3. How much does she spend/save? 4. How much is a new record-player? 5. How much has Liz got? 6. Where do people sometimes sell record-players? 7. Are they expensive?
(Lines 17-29): 8. What's Mrs Carter's telephone number? 9. How much is her record-player? 10. Can you play stereo records on it? 11. When can Liz and her father go and look at it? 12. Where does Mrs Carter live?
(Lines 30-37): 13. What's Liz's problem? 14. How can Liz's father help her? → Ex 10

8 Ex

1 *Make questions.*

1. <u>Do you go to school</u> by bike? — No, I don't. I go to school by bus.
2. ... lunch at school? — Yes, I do. I usually eat lunch at school.
3. ... after school? — No, I don't go to a school club.
4. ... with your father? — No, I don't. I do my homework with my mother.
5. ... French at school? — Yes, we learn French at school.
6. ... French lessons? — Yes, I like them. They're very interesting.
7. ... cassettes? — Yes, we listen to French cassettes.
8. ... books? — No, I don't. But I read French comics.

2 *What do they do with their pocket-money? — Write short dialogues.*

1. Do you get pocket-money, Sally?
   — Yes, I do.
   Do you get it every month?
   — Yes.
   How much do you get?
   — £8.
   How much do you save?
   — Nothing.
   What do you buy with your money?
   — Well, I buy cassettes, magazines and records.

2. ... pocket-money, Carol?
   — Yes, ...
   ... it every month?
   — No. I ... every week.
   How ... you get?
   — ...
   How ... save?
   — I save ... a week.
   ... with your money?
   — Well, ... records, felt-tips, ...

3. 4.

Go on.

3 *Use these verbs and complete the dialogues:* **watch   work   do   paint   walk   wash**

1. <u>Does</u> Mr King <u>paint</u> cars?
   — No, he <u>doesn't</u>. He ... houses.
2. ... the Deans ... the housework together?
   — Yes, they ... . They usually ... it at the weekend.
3. ... Sally ... the dishes?
   — Yes, ... She often ... them.
4. ... Mr King ... tennis on Saturday afternoon?
   — No, ... He ... football.
5. ... Dave and Kevin ... to school?
   — Yes, ... They always ... to school together.
6. ... Mrs King and Mrs Connor ... in an office?
   — No, ... They ... at home.

87

8 Ex

4 Let's talk to the children about their free time, their hobbies and their sports. Complete the questions.

1. **What do you do** in your free time, Dave?
   — I play the guitar.
   ... practise?
   — Every afternoon.
   ... practise?
   — In my room.
   ... lessons?
   — Yes, I go to guitar lessons on Wednesdays after school.

2. ... a hobby, Kevin?
   — Yes, I take photos.
   ...?
   — Usually at the weekends.
   ... a photo club?
   — Yes, I go to the school photo club.
   ... meet there?
   — We meet there on Thursdays.

3. ... like sports, Liz?
   — Yes, of course.
   ... play table-tennis?
   — Yes, I do.
   ... play?
   — At school. And sometimes at a friend's house.
   ... a friend's house?
   — Because we haven't got a big table at home.

5 Sorry?

„Wie bitte?" — Stelle dir vor, du hättest die unterstrichenen Wörter nicht verstanden und du möchtest danach fragen.

1. Liz likes <u>photos</u>.
   — Sorry? What does she like?
2. She uses a <u>Japanese</u> camera.
   — Sorry? What ... use?
3. She usually takes <u>black and white</u> photos.
   — Sorry? What photos ...?
4. She goes to the photo club <u>every week</u>.
   — Sorry? How often ...?
5. Mrs Dean works <u>in an office</u>.
   — Sorry? ...?
6. She gets up <u>at six every morning</u>.
   — Sorry? ...?
7. She leaves home <u>at 7.45</u>.
   — Sorry? ...?
8. She does <u>the housework</u> with her husband.
   — Sorry? ...?

6 Simple form or progressive form? — Complete the sentences.

1. Tom usually (drink) coffee, but today he (drink) tea. 2. It (rain) again. It often (rain) here. 3. Where's Dad? - He's in the kitchen. He (make) a cake. He always (make) cakes for guests. 4. Look, there's Kevin. — Yes, he (wait) for Dave. He usually (wait) for him after school. 5. John can't come. He (write) a letter to Sarah. He always (write) to her on her birthday. 6. Where are the boys? — They (play) hockey. They (play) at Woodside Sports Club every Wednesday. 7. I can hear a guitar. — Yes, Dave (practise) with a friend. They (practise) every Friday from six till eight o'clock. 8. Bill can't help you with your bike now. He (work) at Mr Singh's shop. He sometimes (help) Mr Singh on Saturday mornings.

7 Make short dialogues.

1. Dave — play football?
   usually — on Saturday.
   Is Dave **playing** football?
   — Yes, he usually **plays** on Saturday.
2. your friends — still watch TV?
   always — till half past eight.
   Are your friends still **watching** TV?
   — Yes, they always ....
3. Mr Dean — still work?
   often — till seven.
4. Mr Hill — take Sebastian for a walk?
   sometimes - on Saturday afternoons.
5. your little brother — sleep?
   usually - in the afternoon.
6. your parents — work in the garden?
   often — in the summer.
7. Kevin — wait for Dave?
   always — after school.
8. Dr K. Nickel — paint Merlin's rooms again?
   always — on Mondays.

8 *Simple form or progressive form? − Complete the sentences. Be careful with the questions.*

1. No, John isn't at home. He's *practising*. (practise) at his sports club.
   − (he still play) for his school?
2. Can I have your pen for a minute?
   − I'm sorry, but I (use) it.
3. (you sleep)?
   − Oh no! I (read) this book. It's about budgies and other birds. It's interesting. (you often read) books about birds?
4. Look. The sun (shine) and the birds (sing). Let's eat breakfast in the garden.
5. The children are very quiet. What (they do)?
   − Dave (learn) his German words. Sally (tidy up) her room.
6. Merlin can't work in his library. Dr K. Nickel (paint) it.
7. Where (your husband work)?
   − He (work) in a sports shop. (you go) to work, too?
   − No. I (stay) at home and (do) the housework.
8. I usually (sit) next to Tom at school. But today I (sit) next to Dave.
9. Why (Francis bark)? Do you know?
   − He (wait) for his food, I think.
10. (you write) to your pen-friend?
    − Yes, of course. I (not write) letters to other people.

9 **Say it in English:** *beim Einkaufen*

So kannst du in einem Geschäft nach etwas fragen	▶	**I'd like ..., please.** **Do you sell ..., please?** **Have you got ..., please?**
Wenn der Verkäufer dir etwas gibt, sagt er	▶	**Here you are.**
So kannst du nach dem Preis fragen	▶	**How much is it?** **How much are they?**
Oft fragt der Verkäufer, ob du noch etwas haben willst	▶	**Anything else?**

Work with a partner.

1. *Shop assistant:* Can I ... ?
   Kevin: I'd like a ..., please.
   Shop assistant: Here ... .
   Kevin: How much ... ?
   Shop assistant: ... p. ... else?
   Kevin: No, ...

2. *Shop assistant:* Can I ... ?
   Dave: No, ... I'm just ... .

3. *Shop assistant:* ... ?
   Go on.

10 Look at "The record-player" on page 86 again. Now phone one of the people. Write a dialogue.

11 Revision: *long forms – short forms*

1. I am new here.
2. What is that in English?
3. That is the problem.
4. I do not know.
5. We have got no time.
6. We are sorry.
7. Do not be late again.
8. When is your next bus?

I'm new here.
What's that in English?
That's the problem.
I don't know.
We haven't got time.
We're sorry.
Don't be late again.
When's your next bus?

9. My parents are not here.
10. You cannot stay.
11. My mother does not work.
12. He is my best friend.
13. They have got lots of pets.
14. What is your phone number?
15. Kate is not at the club.
16. We do not like the record.

My parents aren't here.
You can't stay.
My mother doesn't work.
He's my best-
They've got lots of
What's your phone
Kate isn't at the c
We don't like
the record

12 Revision: *What do they all do at home, at work or in their free time? – Fill in the missing words. Be careful. In some sentences the verb must have an -s or -es.*

catch   cook   do (2×)   **give   go   make   paint   play   repair** (2×)   **save   take** (2×)
tidy up   watch

1. Lots of people watch TV.
2. Kevin takes photos of animals and people.
3. Merlin does magic.
4. Dr K. Nickel cleans Merlin's rooms every week.
5. Bill repairs broken watches.
6. Pupils do their homework.
7. A mother ... her baby for a walk.
8. Some people play tennis.

9. A cat catches mice.
10. Tim saves his pocket-money.
11. A pop star gives interviews.
12. Mechanics repair cars.
13. John goes to a hockey club.
14. The children make breakfast on Sundays.
15. Mr King often cooks the meals.
16. Mrs King always ... the kitchen.
    tidy up

13 Revision: their   they're   there are
              1   2   3

Fill in the right words.

1. I can't find my cassettes.
   – Look, 3. two on the floor.
2. Why can't you read these books?
   – 1. in Japanese.
3. Do you know these people?
   – Of course. 1. my aunt and my uncle.
4. And the dog?
   – It's Timmy. He's 1. dog.

5. Can I buy these records?
   – Sorry. 2. too expensive.
6. Let's go to the pet shop. 3. some new pets in the window.
7. I must buy a big cage for my hamsters. 1. old cage is too small.
8. 3. no people at the swimming-pool today.
   – Of course not. It's raining.

14 *A MAGIC question game! Ask the right questions.*

1. All MAGICS can play this game.
2. My name is MAGIC.
3. I'm a MAGIC.
4. You must ask me MAGICS.
5. I'm MAGIC years old.
6. I live in a funny MAGIC.
7. A MAGIC lives with me.
8. Sorry, I must do MAGIC now.
9. And at home MAGIC is waiting for me.
10. Dr K. Nickel MAGICS for me, you know.
11. Today he's painting my MAGIC.
12. This week everything is the same colour: MAGIC.

Who can play this game? — All pupils can play it.
What's your name? — Merlin.
What . . . you? — I'm a magician.
What must we . . . ? — Questions.
How old . . . ? — A hundred.
Where . . . ? — In a funny house.
Who — A rabbit.
Do — Magic. Ha! Ha!
What — Dr K. Nickel.
What — He works for me.
What — My library.
What — Yellow.

15 WORDS WORDS WORDS

a *Here are 52 words. Make 13 groups where only "friends" are together. The first word is always the "group word".*

animals autumn bathroom bedroom cake cat chair children crisps club coffee
colours days desk drinks family father food football Friday furniture games
green grey hockey jobs juice June kitchen March May mechanic
Monday months mother mouse park places rabbit red rooms school seasons
shop assistant sofa spring summer Sunday tea teacher tennis toast

1. animals   2. drinks   3. *?*   4. family   5. places   6. months   7. rooms
   rabbit   tennis   tea   father   club   May   kitchen
   cat   football   juice   mother   school   March   bathroom
   mouse   hockey   coffee   children   park   June   bedroom

8. jobs   9. colours 10. furniture 11. food   12. days   13. season
   teacher   green   sofa   cake   Friday   autumn
   mechanic   grey   desk   crisps   Monday   summer
   shop   red   chair   toast   Sunday   spring
   assistant

b *Small letters or CAPITAL LETTERS? – Welche Wörter haben immer große Anfangsbuchstaben?*

DECEMBER COMIC I YOU HATFIELD TOWN VILLAGE ENGLISH GERMAN
BRITISH BRITAIN INDIA STREET GERMANY FRIDAY HOBBY SPRING
SUMMER SUNDAY MORNING AFTERNOON MAY WEEKEND QUIZ TOM

Finde mindestens zehn weitere Wörter, die immer groß geschrieben werden.

c *German: "bitte"* → *English: "please" – "You're welcome." – "Here you are." – "Sorry?"*

1. Thank you for your help.
   — *You're welcome*
2. Can I talk to Sarah, *please*.
   — *Sorry?* I can't hear you.
3. Can I have your new cassette?
   — *Here you are*
   Thank you.
4. Can I help you?
   — Yes, *please*.

16 Listening comprehension: The baby rabbit

8 Ex

17 Sounds

bag, Dave, grass, sofa, anything, always, after, crazy, father, happy, watch, match, orange, past, place, radio, small, village, wash, woman, tall, another, Sally, what, many

[æ] bag, …	[ɑː] grass, …	[ɒ] …	[ɪ] …
[eɪ] Dave, …	[ə] sofa, …	[ɔː] …	[e] …

mother, dog, so, do, come, welcome, problem, women, clock, balcony, poster, some, two, of course, don't, who, Tom, money, over, ten to three

[ʌ] mother, …	[əʊ] so, …	[uː] …
[ɒ] dog, …	[ə] …	[ɪ] …

Was sage ich, wenn …

… ich wissen will, was ein Wort bedeutet?	What does "lively" mean, please?
… ich möchte, dass der Lehrer ein Wort buchstabiert?	Can you spell "lively", please?
… ich wissen will, wie man etwas ausspricht?	How do you pronounce the second word in line 12, please?

Song: My Bonnie

My Bon-nie is o-ver the o-cean,— my Bon-nie is o-ver the sea,— my Bon-nie is o-ver the o-cean,— oh bring back my Bon-nie to me!— Bring back, bring back, oh bring back my Bon-nie to me, to me, bring back, bring back, oh bring back my Bon-nie to me!—

Just for fun

1. Six girls are walking to school. They've only got one umbrella[1], but they aren't wet? Why not?
2. What's in London *and* in Germany?
3. There's a family with ten brothers. Every brother has got a sister. How many children are there in the family?
4. There are 60 seconds in a minute. How many seconds are there in a year?

[1] umbrella *Regenschirm*

It eats pupils for breakfast

Mr Hill: Good afternoon, boys and girls.
Class: Good afternoon, Mr Hill.
Mr Hill: Liz, what are you doing? Are you reading comics again? We've got English now.
Liz: Sorry, sir. But it's the school magazine. There are some questions in it about our hobbies. One question is "What do you do in your free time?"
Mr Hill: I hope you do your homework.
Kevin: What do you do in *your* free time, Mr Hill?
Mr Hill: I read your homework. And it's sometimes terrible.
Liz: Another question is "Have you got a strange hobby?"
Sandra: My mother has got a strange hobby, Mr Hill. She collects plants. We must have a hundred plants in the house. And she talks to them. Every morning she goes to her plants and says, "Oh, you're a good rubber plant. You're very nice today. Here's some nice water for you."

Kevin: She's crazy.
Mr Hill: No, she isn't.
Kevin: Well, I think she is.

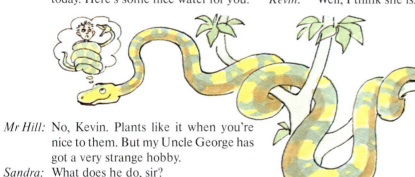

Mr Hill: No, Kevin. Plants like it when you're nice to them. But my Uncle George has got a very strange hobby.
Sandra: What does he do, sir?
Mr Hill: He collects pets.
Liz: That isn't very strange.
Mr Hill: Ah, but the pets are strange. One is very, very long. It's, oh, three metres long. It's brown, yellow and blue — and it eats pupils for breakfast. I can bring it tomorrow and you can see it.
Class: Oh no!
Kevin: What is it, sir?
Mr Hill: It's a boa constrictor.
Dave: What's a boa constrictor?
Mr Hill: Well, you can ask me again tomorrow before it eats you. ... OK. Where are your books? Let's look at page 79 ...

(Lines 1–26): 1. What's Liz reading? 2. What does Mr Hill do in his free time? 3. What does Sandra's mother do with her plants? 4. Does Mr Hill think that Sandra's mother is crazy?
(Lines 27–44): 5. Why is Uncle George's hobby strange? 6. What does Uncle George's pet eat in the mornings? 7. Do you think this is right? 8. When can the pupils see the boa constrictor?

1 Wortstellung (Word order)

a in Nebensätzen (in subordinate clauses)

Subordinate clauses

		Subject	Verb	Object
I usually buy sweets	**when**	I	get	my pocket-money.
The sports club is the place	**where**	Sandra	plays	hockey.
Kevin can't play	**because**	he	has got	an invitation to a party.

In Nebensätzen (die z.B. durch *when, where* oder *because* eingeleitet werden) bleibt die Wortstellung **Subject – Verb – Object** erhalten: S – V – O ... when *I get* my pocket-money. Vergleiche die Wortstellung in deutschen Nebensätzen: „..., wenn *ich* mein Taschengeld *bekomme* ".

b in Fragen (in questions)

			Subject	Verb	Object
Mit *can*:	Kevin and Carol **can** speak French.	**Can**	Kevin and Carol	speak	French?
Im *simple present*:	Kevin and Carol speak French.	**Do**	Kevin and Carol	speak	French?

Im Englischen werden Fragen mit Hilfe eines Hilfsverbs gebildet (z.B. *can*).
Für Fragen im *simple present* verwenden wir eine Form des Hilfsverbs *do*. Die Wortstellung S – V – O bleibt.

2 The simple present in questions

a Yes/No questions and short answers

Do	I you we you they	**speak** English?	Yes,	I you we you they	**do**.	No,	I you we you they	**don't**.
Does	he she it			he she it	**does**.		he she it	**doesn't**.

⚠ Carol speak**s** French.
Doe**s** Carol speak French?

b Questions with question words

Question words	Auxiliary	Subject	Main verb	
(What	**can**	you	see?)	
Where	**do**	you	go	on Saturday afternoons?
Why	**do**	Dave and Kevin	walk	to school?
What	**does**	Liz	play	in her free time?
How often	**does**	Sandra	watch	TV?
When	**do**	you	do	your homework?

⚠ Auch wenn *do* Vollverb ist (deutsch: *machen, tun*), wird die Frage mit dem Hilfsverb *do* gebildet:
When **do you do** your homework? → Wann **machst du** deine Hausaufgaben?

3 The simple present and the present progressive

Simple present	Present progressive

Dave King **goes** to Park School.

Look, Dave **is going** to school.

Mr King **leaves** home at eight o'clock **every day**.

It's Monday morning. Mr King **is leaving** home **now**. What time is it?

Sandra **sometimes drinks** tea with her breakfast. She **never drinks** coffee.

Today Sandra **isn't drinking** tea. She**'s drinking** orange juice.

Does Kevin **often take** photos?
— Yes, he **does**.

Is Kevin **taking** a photo **at the moment**?
— Yes, he **is**.

What **do** you **do on Saturday afternoons**, Liz?
I **usually play** table-tennis.

What**'s** Liz **doing this afternoon**?
— She**'s watching** TV.

Wir verwenden das *simple present*, wenn jemand etwas regelmäßig, üblicherweise, oft, immer oder nie tut.

In Sätzen mit dem *simple present* finden wir häufig Wörter wie:
every day, sometimes, usually, often, always, never, on Saturdays.

Wir verwenden das *present progressive*, wenn jemand etwas im Augenblick/gerade tut. Die Handlung ist noch nicht abgeschlossen, sie ist noch im Gange.

In Sätzen mit dem *present progressive* finden wir häufig Wörter wie:
now, today, at the moment, this afternoon.

 Es gibt eine Reihe von Verben (z.B. *hear, know, like, see, think, understand*), die normalerweise nicht im *present progressive* verwendet werden.

Nach dem Weg fragen; den Weg beschreiben

1 Excuse me, where's the hospital, please?
— It's in Mill Road.

hospital

hotel

station

Excuse me, can you tell me the way to the hospital, please?

— Sorry, I don't know.

— Yes. Go along Grove Street.
Turn left into Mill Road.
Go along Mill Road.
Go across Roman Road.
The hospital is on the right.

Thank you.

go along . . .

9A

 t office
 church
 police station
 cinema
 bank

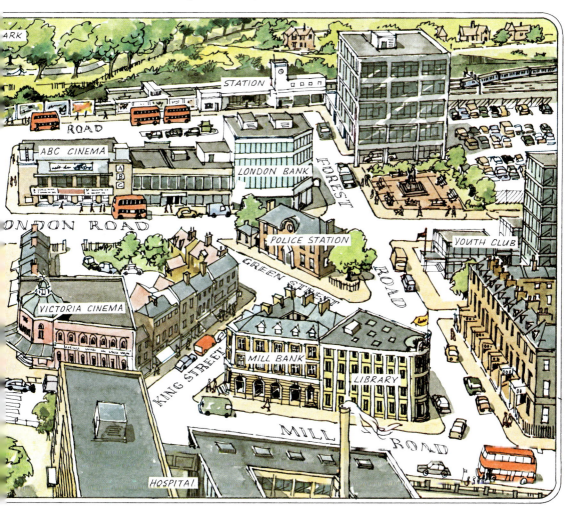

 left into ...
 turn right into ...
... on the left
... on the right

9 A Über den Wohnort sprechen

2 Liz has got a pen-friend in Germany.
Liz is writing to her now.
This is her letter.

9 Woodside Road
Hatfield
June 14th

Dear Anja,

Thank you for your letter. Yes, I can tell you about Hatfield. It's a small town 20 miles from London. About 30,000 people live here, I think. There's old Hatfield and new Hatfield. I live in the new town. And, of course, there's Hatfield House. That's a very big, old house with an interesting history. You can visit the house and look at some of the rooms. It's very popular with tourists. The house has got beautiful gardens and it's in a huge park. Hatfield Park is a great place. My friends and I often go and play in the park in the summer.
The town centre is boring. I don't like it. There are only shops and a square with a fountain. We sometimes meet at the fountain after school or on Saturday afternoons. At least it's quiet because there are no cars or buses – it's a pedestrian precinct. Oh, and we've got a youth club where we can go in the evenings. It's not bad. And there's a super modern swimming-pool in Hatfield. Have you got a nice swimming-pool in your town? Can you swim?
Write and tell me about your town. Is it very big? Are there lots of interesting things? Please write soon!

Love,

Liz

P.S. Do you like my photo of the fountain?

Write a letter about your town.

What's interesting in your town?	We've got a church/... in our town. It's very old/interesting. There's a .... It's .... There are some .... They're ....
What do you like in your town?	I like the .... I think it's nice/modern/big/...
What don't you like?	I don't like the ... because it's terrible/noisy/too small.

Über Ferien sprechen

9A

3. Britain is an island. No town is more than 75 miles (120 kilometres) from the sea. In the summer people often go to the coast. They go there at the weekend. Or they go there on holiday. There are lots of good beaches along the British coast, but the sea is never very warm.

4. Of course, people don't only go to the sea. There are lots of lakes, mountains and rivers, too.

5. **What can you do when you're on holiday?**

... lie on the beach

... swim in a lake

... climb mountains

... buy postcards and souvenirs

Some people lie on the beach.
Some people ...
...

Where can you stay?

hotel

guest house

youth hostel

camp site

Some people stay at a hotel.
Some people ...

And some people stay at home.

99

9T Come and see Britain

There are lots of interesting sights in Britain. Tourists often visit one of the famous old towns. They can walk along the old streets and look at the houses, churches and museums.

This is York, for example. In the picture you can see the Minster.

Chester is another interesting old town. It is near Liverpool. It has got very nice black and white houses. This is a street with shops in the centre of Chester.

Of course, lots of tourists go to London and visit Buckingham Palace. You can look at Buckingham Palace from the outside, but you cannot go in and drink a cup of tea with the Queen!

Castles in Britain are often on a hill or near the coast. This is Caernarfon Castle, one of the many in Wales. It is about 700 years old.

Another nice place for tourists is Cornwall. This is Tintagel Castle. Some people say it is the home of King Arthur and his men.

Loch Ness is one of the beautiful lakes in Scotland. The word for lake in Scotland is "loch". Every year tourists go to Loch Ness and wait for the monster, but not many people see "Nessie". You can swim in the lakes, but the water is *very* cold.

Activity

Find all these places on a map. Collect pictures or postcards of other sights in Britain.

Quiz about the book

A. Who are they?

1. He has got two sisters.
2. He has got a pet shop.
3. They always argue.
4. He paints Merlin's rooms.
5. Francis is their dog.
6. He has got an orange dining-room.
7. He can lift a car.
8. She works in an office.
9. Mozart is his cat's name.
10. He has got a pet – it's brown and yellow and very long!

B. Who says . . . ?

1. "Here you are, little brother."
2. "It's my record-player and it's my birthday."
3. "There's a very nice café near here."
4. "You can have a new room — in the garage."
5. "You can stay at home and listen to your records."

C. What . . .

1. is the first meal of the day?
2. is Woodside?
3. is Mr King's job?
4. are the first, the fifth and the eighth months of the year?
5. can you collect?

D. When . . .

1. does school start in Britain?
2. does school finish in Britain?
3. do pupils go to clubs?
4. do pupils do their homework?
5. has February got 29 days?
6. has April got 29 days?
7. does Tom arrive? —
   He leaves home every day at 8.15. He walks to the bus (4 minutes). He waits for the bus (5 minutes). He sits in the bus (15 minutes). He walks to school (3 minutes). He talks to some friends (5 minutes). He goes to his classroom (3 minutes).

E. Who are they and what are they doing?

F. Britain

1. Where is Hatfield?
2. Where is Kevin from?
3. Edinburgh is in . . . .
4. Nessie lives in . . . .
5. Caernarfon is in . . . .
6. Where does the Queen live?

Just for fun

Can you say this?

She sells shells[1].
She sells sea-shells.
She sells sea-shells
on the sea-shore[2].

[1] shell *Muschel*   [2] sea-shore *Strand*

The English alphabet

a [eɪ]	d [diː]	g [dʒiː]	j [dʒeɪ]	m [em]	p [piː]	s [es]	v [viː]	y [waɪ]
b [biː]	e [iː]	h [eɪtʃ]	k [keɪ]	n [en]	q [kjuː]	t [tiː]	w [ˈdʌbljuː]	z [zed]
c [siː]	f [ef]	i [aɪ]	l [el]	o [əʊ]	r [ɑː]	u [juː]	x [eks]	

English sounds

iː	tea, we, sweets	ʊ	book, good	p	pen, pupil, cup	s	six, December, yes
ɑː	class, car	ə	again, sister, terrible	b	bike, table, Bob	z	present, his
ɔː	or, small, four	eɪ	eight, name, play	t	ten, bottle, sit	ʃ	she, washes, English
uː	two, blue, room	aɪ	my, time	d	dog, window, record	tʃ	children, teacher, watch
ɜː	work, her, first	ɔɪ	boy, toilet	k	car, packet, book	dʒ	Jim, cages, garage
ɪ	in, big	əʊ	only, no, yellow	g	good, again, dog	ŋ	painting, evening
e	yes, pen	aʊ	now, house	l	like, old, small	θ	three, youth club, month
æ	black, cat	ɪə	here, we're, near	r	ruler, children, dry	ð	the, father, with
ʌ	rubber, bus	eə	there, repair, wear	v	very, November, save	j	yes, you
ɒ	on, dog, watch	ʊə	you're, poor	w	we, homework, one	ʒ	television

ˈ = Betonung; die Betonungsstriche stehen immer **vor** der betonten Silbe
‿ = zwei Wörter werden beim Sprechen aneinander gebunden

Grammatical terms

auxiliary [ɔːˈzɪljəri]	Hilfsverb
definite article [ˈdefɪnɪt ˈɑːtɪkl]	bestimmter Artikel
indefinite article [ɪnˈdefɪnɪt ˈɑːtɪkl]	unbestimmter Artikel
imperative [ɪmˈperətɪv]	Imperativ
infinitive [ɪnˈfɪnɪtɪv]	Infinitiv
-ing form	-ing-Form
main verb [ˈmeɪn ˈvɜːb]	Vollverb
negative imperative [ˈnegətɪv ɪmˈperətɪv]	verneinter Imperativ
negative sentence [ˈnegətɪv ˈsentəns]	verneinter Satz
noun [naʊn]	Nomen
object [ˈɒbdʒɪkt]	Objekt
object form	Personalpronomen im Dativ und Akkusativ
person [ˈpɜːsn]	Person
personal pronoun [ˈpɜːsənl ˈprəʊnaʊn]	Personalpronomen
plural [ˈplʊərəl]	Plural
positive sentence [ˈpɒzɪtɪv ˈsentəns]	Aussagesatz
possessive adjective [pəˈzesɪv ˈædʒɪktɪv]	adjektivisch gebrauchtes Possessivpronomen
possessive form [pəˈzesɪv]	Genitiv, besitzanzeigende Form
present progressive [ˈpreznt prəˈgresɪv]	Verlaufsform des Präsens
question word [ˈkwestʃən wɜːd]	Fragewort, Interrogativpronomen
short answer [ˈʃɔːt ˈɑːnsə]	Kurzantwort
simple present [ˈsɪmpl ˈpreznt]	einfache Form des Präsens
singular [ˈsɪŋgjʊlə]	Singular
subject [ˈsʌbdʒɪkt]	Subjekt
subordinate clause [səˈbɔːdnət ˈklɔːz]	Nebensatz
verb [vɜːb]	Verb; Prädikat
word order [ˈwɜːd ˈɔːdə]	Wortstellung, -folge
yes/no question	Entscheidungsfrage

Names

Families

Bell [bel]
Carter ['kɑːtə]
Connor ['kɒnə]
Cooper ['kuːpə]
Dean [diːn]
Doyle [dɔɪl]
Easton ['iːstən]
Hill [hɪl]
Homer ['həʊmə]
Hooley ['huːlɪ]
Johnson ['dʒɒnsn]
Jones [dʒəʊnz]
King [kɪŋ]
Miller ['mɪlə]
Nickel ['nɪkl]
Pitt [pɪt]
Sales [seɪlz]
Singh [sɪŋ]
Walker ['wɔːkə]

Boys/men

Alan ['ælən]
Albert ['ælbət]
Andy ['ændɪ]
Bill(y) ['bɪlɪ]
Bob [bɒb]
Dave [deɪv]
Francis ['frɑːnsɪs]
George [dʒɔːdʒ]
Henry ['henrɪ]
Jack [dʒæk]
Jerry ['dʒerɪ]
Jim(my) ['dʒɪmɪ]
John [dʒɒn]
Kevin ['kevɪn]
Mark [mɑːk]
Martin ['mɑːtɪn]
Mike [maɪk]
Nick [nɪk]
Paul [pɔːl]
Peter ['piːtə]
Sebastian [sɪ'bæstjən]
Simon ['saɪmən]
Terry ['terɪ]
Tim(my) ['tɪmɪ]
Toby ['təʊbɪ]
Tom [tɒm]

Girls/women

Anne [æn]
Carol ['kærəl]
Clare [kleə]
Jane [dʒeɪn]
Janet ['dʒænɪt]
Jenny ['dʒenɪ]
Jill [dʒɪl]
Judy ['dʒuːdɪ]
Karen ['kærən]
Kate [keɪt]
Kelly ['kelɪ]
Liz(zy) ['lɪzɪ]
Mary ['meərɪ]
Pam [pæm]
Pat [pæt]
Sally ['sælɪ]
Sandra ['sændrə]
Sarah ['seərə]
Sheena ['ʃiːnə]
Susan ['suːzn]
Susie ['suːzɪ]
Tina ['tiːnə]

Place names

Belfast [bel'fɑːst]
Dover ['dəʊvə]
Edinburgh ['edɪnbərə]
Hamburg ['hæmbɜːg]
Hatfield ['hætfiːld]
London ['lʌndən]
Manchester ['mæntʃɪstə]
Oxford ['ɒksfəd]
Watford ['wɒtfəd]
Woodside ['wʊdsaɪd]
York [jɔːk]

Andrew Way ['ændruː 'weɪ]
Caernarfon Castle [kə'nɑːvn 'kɑːsl]
Grove Road ['grəʊv 'rəʊd]
Park School ['pɑːk 'skuːl]
Potters Park ['pɒtəz 'pɑːk]
Redway Road ['redweɪ 'rəʊd]
Roman Road ['rəʊmən 'rəʊd]
Smith Road ['smɪθ 'rəʊd]

Other names

Blacky ['blækɪ]
Merlin ['mɜːlɪn]
Mozart ['məʊtsɑːt]
Peanut ['piːnʌt]
Pluto ['pluːtəʊ]
Prince [prɪns]
Rumpelstiltskin [rʌmpl'stɪltskɪn]
Tabby ['tæbɪ]
Wag [wæg]

Anmerkungen zum Vocabulary

In der **ersten Spalte** des folgenden Wörterverzeichnisses (Vocabulary) sind die neuen Wörter jeder Unit aufgeführt. Die einzigen Ausnahmen sind grammatikalische Fachausdrücke und Eigennamen, die auf den Seiten 103 und 104 jeweils gesammelt aufgeführt sind. Die **fett gedruckten** Wörter sollst du beim eigenen Sprechen und Schreiben verwenden können; sie gehören zum so genannten produktiven Wortschatz. Die **normal gedruckten** Wörter sollst du verstehen, wenn du sie hörst oder liest; sie gehören zum so genannten rezeptiven Wortschatz*. Die **kursiv gedruckten** Wörter brauchst du dir nicht zu merken, da sie in den folgenden Units nicht als bekannt vorausgesetzt werden.
Alle Wörter der ersten Spalte werden in ihrer Grundform aufgeführt, d.h. die Nomen in der Regel im Singular, die Verben in der Infinitivform, die durch vorangestelltes (to) zusätzlich gekennzeichnet ist. Die Hinzufügung **sb.** (= some**b**ody) entspricht der deutschen Abkürzung jn. (= jemanden) bzw. jm. (= jemandem); **sth.** (= some**th**ing) heißt auf Deutsch „etwas".
Wie du die Wörter aussprechen musst, kannst du der **Lautschrift** in den eckigen Klammern [ ] entnehmen; eine Erklärung der Symbole findest du auf Seite 103.
In der **zweiten Spalte** stehen die **deutschen Bedeutungen** der englischen Wörter.
In der **dritten Spalte** geben wir Hinweise, die dir zeigen, wie man die englischen Wörter richtig verwendet; zum Teil sind es **Beispielsätze**, aber darüber hinaus haben wir dort in Kästchen Wörtergruppen oder Ausdrücke – oft aus verschiedenen Units – zusammengefasst, damit du ihre Gemeinsamkeiten und Unterschiede auf einen Blick erkennen kannst. Wir hoffen, dass sie dir das Vokabellernen erleichtern.

*In Bundesländern, in denen keine Unterscheidung zwischen produktivem und rezeptivem Wortschatz gemacht wird, sollten alle Wörter gleich behandelt werden.

Vocabulary

Introduction

p.5 introduction [ɪntrə'dʌkʃn] — Einführung, Einleitung
here's [hɪəz] — hier ist
  = **here is** [hɪər ɪz]
it's [ɪts] — es ist
  = **it is** [ɪt ɪz]
a [ə] — ein, eine
town [taʊn] — Stadt
in [ɪn] — in
England ['ɪŋglənd] — England
near [nɪə] — in der Nähe von, nahe (bei)

Here's London.
It's a town in England.

Bochum is *near* Essen.

p.6 **Hallo.** [hə'ləʊ] — Hallo! (Guten) Tag!
I'm [aɪm] — ich bin
  = **I am** [aɪ æm]
I'm from Bonn. — Ich bin/komme aus Bonn.
  [aɪm frəm 'bɒn]
from [frɒm, frəm] — aus; von
new [nju:] — neu
and [ænd, ənd, ən] — und
you [ju:, jʊ] — du

Hallo, Dave. – *Hallo*, Liz.
I'm Sabine Müller. *I'm* eleven.

Kevin is *new* in Hatfield. *And* I'm *new* in Stuttgart.

p.7 **activity** [æk'tɪvəti] — Projekt, Beschäftigung
Germany ['dʒɜ:məni] — Deutschland
song [sɒŋ] — Lied
round [raʊnd] — Kanon
my [maɪ] — mein, meine

"Alle Vögel sind schon da" is a *song* from *Germany*.

I'm from Dortmund. Dortmund is *my* town.

Unit 1

1 **unit** ['ju:nɪt] — Lektion, Lehrbucheinheit
Good morning. — Guten Morgen! Guten Tag!
  [gʊd 'mɔ:nɪŋ]
good [gʊd] — gut
morning ['mɔ:nɪŋ] — Morgen, Vormittag
Mr Hill ['mɪstə] — Herr Hill
your [jɔ:, jə] — dein(e); Ihr(e); euer, eure
English ['ɪŋglɪʃ] — englisch; Engländer, Engländerin; Englisch
teacher ['ti:tʃə] — Lehrer, Lehrerin
class [klɑ:s] — Klasse

Good morning, Mr Hill.

Here's *your* teacher, Kevin. = … *dein* Lehrer
Here's *your* new class, Mr Hill. = … *Ihre* neue Klasse
Here's *your* teacher, Jane and Tom. = … *euer* Lehrer

Dave is *English*. = Dave ist Engländer.

Mr Hill is a *teacher*. = Mr Hill ist Lehrer.
Liz is in *class* 1F.

2 **How old are you?** — Wie alt bist du?
  [haʊ 'əʊld ə 'ju:]
Where are you from? — Wo kommst du her?
  ['weər ə jʊ 'frɒm]
Where? [weə] — Wo?
Ask a partner. — Frag(t) einen Partner/eine Partnerin!
  ['ɑ:sk ə 'pɑ:tnə]

How old are you? – Eleven.

Where are you from? – I'm from Germany. From Mainz.

Where's Hatfield? = *Where is* Hatfield? – It's in England.

3 **yes** [jes] — ja
no [nəʊ] — nein
What's your name? — Wie ist dein Name? Wie heißt du?
  ['wɒts jə 'neɪm]
  = **What is …?**
What? [wɒt] — Was?
not [nɒt] — nicht
but [bʌt, bət] — aber
brother ['brʌðə] — Bruder

What's your name? – Katrin.
My name is Katrin./*I'm* Katrin. = Ich heiße Katrin.

1 A 4	you're [juə, jɔː]	du bist; Sie sind; ihr seid
	= you are [juːɑː]	
	sister ['sɪstə]	Schwester
	That's right. [raɪt]	Das ist richtig. Stimmt!
	that's … [ðæts]	das ist …
	= that is …	
1 A 5	pupil ['pjuːpl]	Schüler, Schülerin
	at school [ət 'skuːl]	in der Schule
	German ['dʒɜːmən]	deutsch; Deutsche, Deutscher; Deutsch
1 A 6	tall [tɔːl]	groß *(bei Menschen)*; hoch
	small [smɔːl]	klein
	he's [hiːz]	er ist
	= he is [hiːɪz]	
	she's [ʃiːz]	sie ist
	= she is [ʃiːɪz]	
	he/she isn't ['ɪznt]	er/sie ist nicht
	= he/she is not	
	…, too. [tuː]	auch
	quiet ['kwaɪət]	still, ruhig, leise
	lively ['laɪvlɪ]	lebhaft
	boy [bɔɪ]	Junge
	girl [gɜːl]	Mädchen
	the [ðə]	der, die, das; die *(Plural)*
	rabbit ['ræbɪt]	Kaninchen
	very ['verɪ]	sehr
	nice [naɪs]	nett, schön, hübsch
1 A 8	his [hɪz]	sein, seine
	her [hɜː, hə]	ihr, ihre
1 A 9	the same [seɪm]	der-, die-, dasselbe; dieselben
	they're [ðeə]	sie sind
	= they are [ðeɪɑː]	
	they aren't [ɑːnt]	sie sind nicht
	= they are not	
	friend [frend]	Freund, Freundin
	of course [əv 'kɔːs]	natürlich, selbstverständlich
1 A 10	we're [wɪə]	wir sind
	= we are [wiːɑː]	

○ **Song**

	chorus ['kɔːrəs]	Refrain
1 Ex 1	exercise ['eksəsaɪz]	Übung, Übungsaufgabe
	Say it in English. [seɪ]	Sag(t) es auf Englisch!
	Good afternoon.	Guten Tag! *(nachmittags)*

Are *you* in class 1F, Dave? = Bist *du* … ?
Are *you* from Hatfield, Mr Hill? = Sind *Sie* … ?
Are *you* English, Sandra and Sally? = Seid *ihr* … ?

Mr Hill is my new teacher. — Oh, *that's* good.

Liz is *at Park School.* = Liz *geht auf die Park School.*
Liz is *at school.* = Liz ist (jetzt) *in der Schule.*

I'm *German.*
= Ich bin Deutsche/Deutscher.

Sandra is *tall,*
but Liz is *small.*

Kevin is eleven and Sandra is eleven, *too.*
Liz is *quiet.* She isn't *lively.*

Your English is *very* good.

Tom is lively. But *his* brother is quiet.
Sally and *her* brother are at Park School.

Kevin is in class 1F. But Sally isn't in *the same* class.

They're German, they *aren't* English.

Is Liz English? — Yes, *of course.* *Of course* she's English.

I	= ich
you	= du
he	= er
she	= sie
it	= es (er, sie)
we	= wir
you	= ihr, Sie
they	= sie

English—German
What's "rabbit" *in German?* = … auf Deutsch?
"Partner" is a word *in English* and *in German.* = … im Englischen …
Anne is my *English* friend. = … meine englische Freundin.
Frau Schulze is my *English* teacher. = … meine Englischlehrerin.
Her *English* is very good. = Ihr Englisch …
But she's *German,* of course. = … sie ist Deutsche …

	afternoon [ˌɑːftəˈnuːn]	Nachmittag
	evening [ˈiːvnɪŋ]	Abend
	Goodbye. [gʊdˈbaɪ]	Auf Wiedersehen!
	Bye. [baɪ]	Wiedersehen! Tschüs!
	Miss Black [mɪs]	Fräulein/Frau Black (Anrede für unverheiratete Frauen)
	role-play [ˈrəʊlpleɪ]	Rollenspiel
3	Ask a **question**. [ˈkwestʃən]	Stell(t) eine Frage!
6	combination exercise [kɒmbɪˈneɪʃn]	Kombinationsübung, Zuordnungsübung
7	(to) fill in [fɪlˈɪn]	einsetzen
10	**word** [wɜːd]	Wort
11	**short** [ʃɔːt]	kurz
	long [lɒŋ]	lang
	form [fɔːm]	Form
12	sound [saʊnd]	Laut, Ton; Klang
w	**for** [fɔː, fə]	für
S	(to) **be** [biː, bɪ]	sein

Unit 2

1	**family** (Pl.: **families**) [ˈfæmɪlɪ]	Familie
	this is … [ðɪs ɪz]	dies/das (hier) ist …
	Mrs King [ˈmɪsɪz]	Frau King
	father [ˈfɑːðə]	Vater
	mother [ˈmʌðə]	Mutter
	parents [ˈpeərənts]	Eltern
2	**I've got** [aɪv ˈgɒt] = I **have got** [hæv ˈgɒt, həv ˈgɒt]	ich habe, ich besitze
	I haven't got [ˈhævnt gɒt] = I **have not got**	ich habe nicht, ich habe keinen/keine/kein
	dog [dɒg]	Hund
	best [best]	bester, beste, bestes
	or [ɔː, ə]	oder
	quiz [kwɪz]	Quiz, Frage-Antwort-Spiel
	Who? [huː]	Wer?
3	he/she **has got** [hæz ˈgɒt, həz ˈgɒt]	er/sie hat
	he/she **hasn't got** [ˈhæznt gɒt] = he/she **has not got**	er/sie hat nicht, er/sie hat keinen/keine/kein
4	**their** [ðeə]	ihr, ihre
	garden [ˈgɑːdn]	Garten
	house [haʊs]	Haus
	big [bɪg]	groß
	garage [ˈgærɑːdʒ]	Garage
	car [kɑː]	Auto, Wagen
	black [blæk]	schwarz
	cat [kæt]	Katze
	on [ɒn]	auf

Die verflixten drei (IHR)

Jill is ten. *Her* brother is eleven. = *Ihr* Bruder …
Where's *your* brother, Mr Hill? = … *Ihr* Bruder …
You're in my class, Peter and Michael. = *Ihr* seid …

Die verflixten vier (SIE)

Klaus and Martin are nice. *They*'re my friends.
Sandra is from Woodside. *She*'s English.
Are *you* my teacher, Mr Hill?
Here's my school. *It*'s very old.

Fill in the right *words*.

"My" is a *short* word, but "introduction" is a *long* word.
"He is" is a long *form*, and "he's" is a short *form*.

The German word *for* "town" is "Stadt".

this/that → it

What's *this*?   — *It*'s a town.
  = Was ist das?   = Das ist eine Stadt.
Is *that* right?   — Yes, *it* is.
What's *that* in English? — *It*'s a school.
  = Wie heißt das auf Englisch?

Have you *got* a brother? — Yes, I *have*. But I haven't got a sister.

a dog   → it
aber mit Namen:
my dog *Ben*   → he
my dog *Susie* → she

Who is Sally? = *Wer* ist Sally?
Where's Sally? = *Wo* ist Sally?

Has Dave King *got* a sister? — Yes, he *has*. = Ja.
Has he *got* a brother? — No, he *hasn't*. = Nein.

They're in *their* garden. = … ihrem Garten.
⚠ They're in *her* garden. = … ihrem Garten.

big = groß und breit: a *big* house/school/dog
tall = groß an Höhe, hoch gewachsen: a *tall* boy/girl

on the car

	balcony (Pl.: balconies) ['bælkənɪ]	Balkon	
	with [wɪð]	mit	
	flat [flæt]	Wohnung	

The Kings have got a house *with* a garden.

2 A 5 at Dave's/my house — bei Dave/mir zu Hause
at home [ət 'həʊm] — zu Hause, daheim
Mum, mum [mʌm] — Mutti, Mama, Mami
Dad, dad [dæd] — Vati, Papa, Papi

> *Where's Sally?*
> *at* Sandra's house *on* the balcony
> *at* home   *in* the house
> *at* school   *in* the garden

2 A 6 white [waɪt] — weiß
fantastic [fæn'tæstɪk] — fantastisch, toll
our ['aʊə] — unser, unsere
young [jʌŋ] — jung
terrible ['terəbl] — schrecklich, furchtbar

We're in class 1F. *Our* teacher is Mr Hill.
Susie is old, but Francis is *young*.
My English is good, but my friend's English is *terrible*.

2 A 7 pen [pen] — Füller; Stift *(außer Bleistift)*
pencil ['pensl] — Bleistift
biro ['baɪrəʊ] — Kugelschreiber, Kuli
felt-tip ['felttɪp] — Filzstift
rubber ['rʌbə] — Radiergummi; Gummi
ruler ['ruːlə] — Lineal
pencil-case ['penslkeɪs] — Federtasche, Federmäppchen
book [bʊk] — Buch
paper, newspaper ['njuːspeɪpə] — Zeitung
magazine [mægə'ziːn] — Zeitschrift, Illustrierte
calculator ['kælkjʊleɪtə] — Taschenrechner
bag [bæg] — Tasche, Beutel, Tüte
number ['nʌmbə] — Zahl, Nummer; Anzahl
game [geɪm] — Spiel

> **Schreibzeug**
> pencil-case   felt-tip
> pen   ruler
> pencil   rubber
> biro

books

bags

2 T pet [pet] — Haustier, Tier (das man sich im Haus hält)
lots (of …) ['lɒts əv] — viele, viel, eine Menge
It's a pity. ['pɪtɪ] — Das ist schade.

A cat is a nice *pet*.
I've got *lots of* friends. Have you got friends, too?
— Yes, *lots*.
We haven't got a pet. *It's a pity.*

2 Ex 1 How are you? [haʊ 'ɑː jʊ] — Wie geht's (dir/Ihnen/euch)?
I'm OK/I'm all right. — Mir geht's gut.
OK = okay [əʊ'keɪ], all right [ɔːl 'raɪt] — gut, in Ordnung
Thank you. ['θæŋkjʊ] — Danke (schön).
Thanks. [θæŋks]
9 colour ['kʌlə] — Farbe
(to) find [faɪnd] — finden

How's Peter? = *How is* Peter?

Here's your book. – *Thank you.*
How are you? - OK, *thanks.*

2 Ww Sorry I'm late. ['sɒrɪ aɪm 'leɪt] — Entschuldigen Sie, dass ich zu spät komme.
(I'm) sorry. — Entschuldigung! Verzeihung! Tut mir Leid!

Have you got a ruler? — No, *I'm sorry.*

2 S its [ɪts] — sein, seine; ihr, ihre *(aber nur bei Sachen und Tieren)*

It's a good school. *Its* teachers are nice.
= Es ist …   = Ihre …

> How are you?   — I'm *all right*, thanks. = Danke, gut.
> Have you got a brother? — Yes, he's terrible. But my sister is *all right*.
>   = … ist ganz in Ordnung.
> Ask a question.   — *All right.* How old are you? = Na gut. …

Unit 3

A1
Saturday ['sætədɪ]	Samstag, Sonnabend	
nine **o'clock** [ə'klɒk]	neun Uhr	
What time is it?	Wie spät ist es?	
time [taɪm]	Zeit	
please [pli:z]	bitte	
Hurry up. [hʌrɪ 'ʌp]	Beeil dich! Beeilt euch!	

What time is it? – It's eleven *o'clock*. It's very late.

What's your name, *please*?
It's late. *Hurry up*, please.

A2
now [naʊ]	jetzt, nun	
problem ['prɒbləm]	Problem, Schwierigkeit	
bike [baɪk]	Fahrrad, Rad	
puncture ['pʌŋktʃə]	Reifenpanne	
Well, ... [wel]	Nun, ...; Also, ...	
Repair it. [rɪ'peər ɪt]	Reparier(t) es/ihn/sie.	
no [nəʊ]	kein, keine	
(to) **help** (sb. with sth.) [help]	(jm. bei etwas) helfen	
me [mi:, mɪ]	mir, mich	

It's three o'clock *now*.
Kevin has got a *problem* with his *bike*.

Please *help* your brother *with* his English exercise.

Help *me*, please.
Ask *me*.

A3
(to) **work** [wɜ:k]	arbeiten
(to) **paint** [peɪnt]	(an)streichen; malen
door [dɔ:]	Tür
shop [ʃɒp]	Laden, Geschäft
(to) **buy** [baɪ]	kaufen
cassette [kə'set]	Cassette
cassette-recorder [kə'setrɪkɔ:də]	Cassettenrecorder
(to) **play** [pleɪ]	spielen

Sandra *is painting*.

Mr King *is painting* the garage door.

A4
(to) **do** [du:, dʊ]	tun, machen

A5
room [ru:m, rʊm]	Zimmer, Raum
He's doing his homework. ['həʊmwɜ:k]	Er macht seine Hausaufgabe(n)/Schularbeiten.
(to) **watch TV**	fernsehen
(to) **watch** sth./sb. [wɒtʃ]	sich etwas ansehen; jm. zuschauen; jn. beobachten
TV [ti:'vi:] = **television** ['telɪvɪʒn]	Fernsehen, Fernseher
match [mætʃ]	Spiel, Wettkampf, Match

Homework is terrible. *(Kein Plural!)*

Dave and Sally *are watching TV*. They're watching a tennis match.
Mr Connor is playing tennis, and Kevin *is watching*.
Sandra *is watching* Wag. He's playing with Dave.
The Connors have got a new *TV*. Now they're watching *TV*.

7
still [stɪl]	(immer) noch
(to) **read** [ri:d]	lesen; vorlesen
(to) **listen to** sth./sb. ['lɪsn tʊ, tə]	sich etwas anhören; jm. zuhören, auf jn. hören
(to) **clean** [kli:n]	putzen, reinigen
repair shop [rɪ'peə ʃɒp]	Reparaturwerkstatt für Fahrräder

Are Kevin and Carol *still* playing? – Yes, they're *still* in the garden.

> **no/not a = kein, keine**
> (It's) *no* problem. – (Das ist) kein Problem
> I've got *no* time. = Ich habe keine Zeit.
> We *haven't got a* garden. = Wir haben keinen Garten.
> This is a pen. It *isn't a* pencil. = Es ist kein Bleistift.

9
(to) **be on the (tele)phone** ['telɪfəʊn]	am Telefon sein, gerade telefonieren
(to) **talk** to sb. [tɔ:k]	mit jm. sprechen, reden; sich mit jm. unterhalten
(to) be **hungry** ['hʌŋgrɪ]	hungrig sein, Hunger haben
(to) **wait for** sb. [weɪt]	auf jn. warten
you [ju:, jʊ]	dir, Ihnen, euch; dich, Sie, euch

Sandra *is talking to* Liz. The two girls *are talking*.

I'm very *hungry*. = Ich habe großen Hunger.

109

3 A 10	together [təˈgeðə]	zusammen, miteinander	
	I'm on my way (to …). [weɪ]	Ich bin auf dem Weg/ unterwegs (nach/zu …).	
	to [tuː, tʊ, tə]	zu, nach, in	
	swimming-pool [ˈswɪmɪŋpuːl]	Schwimmbad; Schwimmbecken	
	(to) go [gəʊ]	gehen; fahren	
	(to) come, is coming [kʌm]	kommen, mitkommen	
	in a minute	gleich, sofort	
	minute [ˈmɪnɪt]	Minute	
3 A 11	sun [sʌn]	Sonne	
	(to) shine, is shining [ʃaɪn]	scheinen	
	(to) swim, is swimming [swɪm]	schwimmen	
	(to) sit, is sitting [sɪt]	sitzen	
	nothing [ˈnʌθɪŋ]	nichts	
	tired [ˈtaɪəd]	müde	
	(to) sleep [sliːp]	schlafen	
	football [ˈfʊtbɔːl]	Fußball	
	man, men [mæn, men]	Mann, Männer	
	woman, women [ˈwʊmən, ˈwɪmɪn]	Frau, Frauen	

○ **Song**

	bell [bel]	Glocke	
	(to) ring [rɪŋ]	läuten	
3 T	park [pɑːk]	Park	
	(to) go on Mum's bike	mit Muttis Rad fahren	
	It's ten miles to …. [maɪlz]	Es sind zehn Meilen bis (nach/zu) ….	
	later [ˈleɪtə]	später	
	a repair kit [rɪˈpeə kɪt]	(eine Tasche mit) Flickzeug	
	Here you are.	Hier bitte. Bitte sehr.	
	little [ˈlɪtl]	klein, jung	
	with (the girls)	bei (den Mädchen)	
3 Ex 8	answer (to) [ˈɑːnsə]	Antwort (auf eine Frage)	
10	busy [ˈbɪzi]	beschäftigt	
	Go on. [gəʊ ˈɒn]	Mach(t) weiter!	
13	listening comprehension [ˈlɪsnɪŋ kɒmprɪˈhenʃn]	Hörverstehen	
3 Ww	What …?	Was für ein(e) …? Welcher/Welche/Welches …?	
	page [peɪdʒ]	Seite (im Buch)	

Unit 4

4 A 1	people [ˈpiːpl]	Leute, Menschen	
	all [ɔːl]	alle; alles	
4 A 2	Can we have it? [kæn, kən]	Können/Dürfen wir es haben?	

Liz *is on her way* …
… *to* the bookshop. = … zur Buchhandlung.
… *to* Woodside. = … nach Woodside.
… *to* school. = … in die/zur Schule.

Dave *is*
… *going to* … *at the* … *coming from*
the swimming-pool. swimming-pool. the swimming-pool.

Isn't it nice? The *sun is shining.*

Sit down, please. = Bitte setz dich/setzt euch!
Sandra is doing *nothing.* She's *tired.*

Dave has got a new *football.* He's playing *football*
with his friends now.

Isn't my friend helping *you,* Tom? = dir
Isn't my friend helping *you,* Mr Hill? = Ihnen
Isn't my friend helping *you,* Tom and Jim? = euch

I'm waiting for *you,* Anne. = dich
I'm waiting for *you,* Miss Black. = Sie
I'm waiting for *you,* Anne and Kate. = euch

It's 20 miles from Hatfield *to* London.
(*1 mile* = ca. 1,6 km)

Have you got a rubber? — Yes, *here you are.*
⚠ *please* nur bei Fragen und Aufforderungen:
What's that in English, *please*? Help me, *please.*

Kevin, help your sister, please. — Sorry, Dad, I'm *busy.*
I'm painting my bike.

What pets have you got? — A cat and a dog.

What *page* are we on? — We're doing exercise 11
on *page* 34. (Abkürzung: page 34 → p. 34 = S. 34)

The *people* in Hatfield are nice.
Sandra's friends have *all* got pets.
Have you got *all the* bags?

Can't I come? [kɑːnt]		Kann ich nicht (mit)kommen?
too small [tuː]		zu klein
hamster [ˈhæmstə]		Hamster
tonight [təˈnaɪt]		heute Abend, heute Nacht

> The flat is *too* small. = *zu klein*
> The garden is small, *too*. = *auch klein*
> The *two* girls are sisters. = *zwei*

A 3

there's ... [ðəz, ðəz] = **there is** ... [ðeə_ɪz]		da ist ..., es gibt ..., es ist ... (vorhanden)
there are ... [ðeə_ɑː, ðeə_ə]		da sind ..., es gibt ..., es sind ... (vorhanden)
pet shop		Tierhandlung
in Sandfield **Street** [striːt]		in der Sandfield-Straße
owner [ˈəʊnə]		Besitzer, Besitzerin
India [ˈɪndjə]		Indien
(to) **look at** sth.		(sich) etwas anschauen
(to) **look** [lʊk]		sehen, schauen, gucken
window [ˈwɪndəʊ]		Fenster, Schaufenster
budgie [ˈbʌdʒɪ]		Wellensittich
mouse, mice [maʊs, maɪs]		Maus, Mäuse
box (Pl.: **boxes**) [bɒks]		Kiste, Kasten; Schachtel
cage [keɪdʒ]		Käfig
basket [ˈbɑːskɪt]		Korb
some [sʌm, səm]		einige, ein paar; etwas

> **there is   there are**
>
> *There's* a man at the door. = *Da ist ...*
> *Is there* a bookshop near here? = *Gibt es ...?*
> Sorry, *there's* no time for TV. = *Es ist leider ...*
> *There are* no names on the door. = *Es stehen ...*

⚠ We're playing *in the street*. = auf der Straße.

Look at the pets. Aren't they nice?
Look. The rabbit is playing with the calculator.

boxes

He has got *some* questions. = ... einige Fragen
He has got *some* time. = ... etwas Zeit.
Can I help you? — Yes. Have you got a repair kit, please?

A 4

Can I help you?		(*Verkäufer:*) Kann ich Ihnen /dir behilflich sein?
May I go? [meɪ]		Darf ich gehen?
(to) **touch** [tʌtʃ]		berühren, anfassen

May we go now, Mr Hill, please? — Yes, of course.

A 5

You **must** help me. [mʌst, məst]		Du musst mir helfen.
(to) feed [fiːd]		füttern
(to) take the dog for a walk [ˈteɪk ... fər_ə ˈwɔːk]		mit dem Hund rausgehen, mit dem Hund spazieren gehen
every [ˈevrɪ]		jeder, jede, jedes
day [deɪ]		Tag

What *must* we do for homework?
Kevin isn't in his room. He *must* be in the garden.
⚠ Sie *müssen* in die Schule. = They *must go* to school.

⚠ Guten *Tag*! = Hallo; Good morning; Good afternoon.

6

on Monday [ˈmʌndɪ]		am Montag
on Mondays		montags, am Montag
Tuesday [ˈtjuːzdɪ]		Dienstag
Wednesday [ˈwenzdɪ]		Mittwoch
Thursday [ˈθɜːzdɪ]		Donnerstag
Friday [ˈfraɪdɪ]		Freitag
Sunday [ˈsʌndɪ]		Sonntag
It's your turn [tɜːn]		Du bist an der Reihe.
week [wiːk]		Woche

> *on Tuesday* = am Dienstag
> *on Wednesday* afternoon = am Mittwochnachmittag
> *on Sunday* evenings = Sonntag/sonntags abends

A 7

animal [ˈænɪml]		Tier
(to) **hear** [hɪə]		hören
(to) **see** [siː]		sehen
(to) **open** [ˈəʊpən]		öffnen, aufmachen
Be careful. [ˈkeəfl]		Sei(d) vorsichtig!
help [help]		Hilfe
(to) **laugh** [lɑːf]		lachen
only [ˈəʊnlɪ]		nur
funny [ˈfʌnɪ]		lustig, komisch, witzig
favourite [ˈfeɪvrɪt]		Lieblings-
tiger [ˈtaɪgə]		Tiger

> **hear** = hören (können)
> **listen (to)** = zuhören, sich anhören
>
> Can Sandra *hear* me? — Yes, but she *isn't listening*.
> *Listen to* me, please. — Sorry, I can't *hear* you.
> *Listen*. Can you *hear* the car? — No, I'm listening to my cassettes.

> **see   look   watch**
>
> *Look*. Can you *see* the tall boy? He*'s looking at* us.
> *Look at* page 29. Can you *see* Sally and her friends?
> What's Kevin doing? — He*'s watching* a tennis match.

111

4 A 8

(to) bark [bɑːk]	bellen	Listen. Wag *is barking*.
(to) sing [sɪŋ]	singen	
(to) climb [klaɪm]	klettern, steigen	Can you *climb a tree*?
tree [triː]	Baum	= Kannst du auf einen Baum klettern?
(to) fly [flaɪ]	fliegen	
bird [bɜːd]	Vogel	
clever ['klevə]	klug, schlau; *hier:* geschickt	
(to) carry ['kærɪ]	tragen	*Carry* the cassette-recorder to the classroom, please.
thing [θɪŋ]	Ding, Sache	
(to) catch [kætʃ]	fangen, erwischen	

4 A 9

He **can't** swim. [kɑːnt] Er kann nicht schwimmen.
= He **cannot** swim.
['kænɒt, 'kænət]

Kevin *can't* (= *cannot*) be at home. He must be at school.

4 A 10

poor [pʊə, pɔː]	arm	
dream [driːm]	Traum	**Menschen beschreiben**
strong [strɒŋ]	stark; kräftig	old — young, tall — small, quiet — lively, nice — terrible, clever, funny, strong
(to) lift [lɪft]	heben, hochheben	
across [əˈkrɒs]	(quer) über, (quer) durch	across the street 
sea [siː]	Meer	
(to) speak (to sb.) [spiːk]	(mit jm.) sprechen	Can I say it in German? — No, *speak* English, please. (On the phone) Hallo. Can I *speak* to Kevin, please?
French [frentʃ]	französisch; Franzose, Französin; Französisch	⚠ Kannst du Deutsch? = *Can* you *speak* German? Sie kann kein Englisch. = She *can't speak* English.
Japanese [ˌdʒæpəˈniːz]	japanisch; Japaner, Japanerin; Japanisch	
everything ['evrɪθɪŋ]	alles	⚠ You can't have *everything*. (= ein Wort)
home [həʊm]	Heim, Zuhause	You can't play football *every day*. (= zwei Wörter)

○ Song

always ['ɔːlweɪz]	immer	*(to) bend a bar* ['bend ə 'bɑː]	eine Stange (zusammen-) biegen
He's right/wrong. [raɪt, rɒŋ]	Er hat Recht/Unrecht.	*real* [rɪəl]	echt, wirklich
never ['nevə]	nie, niemals	*superman* ['suːpəmæn]	Übermensch, Supermann
He lives ... [lɪvz]	Er wohnt/lebt ...		

4 T

wet [wet]	nass; feucht	Oh, look. The sun isn't shining. It*'s raining*.
(to) rain [reɪn]	regnen	The rabbit is playing with the calculator *again*.
again [əˈgen, əˈgeɪn]	wieder; noch (ein)mal	Your answer isn't right. It's *wrong*.
wrong [rɒŋ]	falsch	
line [laɪn]	Zeile; Linie	

4 Ex 2, 11, 12

picture ['pɪktʃə]	Bild; Aufnahme, Foto	What can you see *in the picture*? = ... auf dem Bild?
(to) try [traɪ]	versuchen, probieren	That's not very good, Peter. *Try* again. = Versuch es noch einmal!
hidden ['hɪdn]	versteckt, verborgen	

4 Ww

(to) explain [ɪkˈspleɪn] erklären, erläutern
toilet ['tɔɪlɪt] Toilette

○ Just for fun

just for fun ['dʒʌst fə 'fʌn]	nur zum Spaß/zum Vergnügen
rhyme [raɪm]	Reim, Vers
rain [reɪn]	Regen
(to) go away [gəʊ əˈweɪ]	weggehen, verschwinden
another day [əˈnʌðə]	an einem anderen Tag
letter ['letə]	Buchstabe
puzzle ['pʌzl]	Rätsel

○ Extra Reading

Junior World ['dʒuːnjə 'wɜːld]	„Junge Welt" *(Name einer Zeitschrift)*
goldfish ['gəʊldfɪʃ]	Goldfisch
you	*hier:* man
lazy ['leɪzɪ]	faul, träge
(to) understand [ˌʌndəˈstænd]	verstehen
(to) write a letter (to sb.) ['raɪt ə 'letə]	einen Brief schreiben (an jn.)

47 The calendar

1. calendar ['kælɪndə] — Kalender
   (to) **make**, is **making** [meɪk] — machen, bauen
   month [mʌnθ] — Monat
   year [jɜː, jɪə] — Jahr
   in **January** ['dʒænjʊərɪ] — im Januar
   February ['febrʊərɪ] — Februar
   March [mɑːtʃ] — März
   April ['eɪprɪl] — April
   May [meɪ] — Mai
   June [dʒuːn] — Juni
   July [dʒuː'laɪ] — Juli
   August ['ɔːgəst] — August
   September [sep'tembə] — September
   October [ɒk'təʊbə] — Oktober
   November [nəʊ'vembə] — November
   December [dɪ'sembə] — Dezember

Buy a box and *make* a house for the rabbit.

1 *year* = 12 *months* = 52 *weeks* = 365 *days*
in 1900 = in (the year) nineteen hundred
in 1988 = in (the year) nineteen eighty-eight
⚠ Er ist zwölf Jahre. = He's twelve *years old*.

4. **What date is it (today)?** — Der Wievielte ist heute? Was ist heute für ein Datum?
   date [deɪt] — Datum
   today [tə'deɪ] — heute
   (to) **write**, is **writing** [raɪt] — schreiben

What date is it on Sunday? – (It's) March 5th.
What day is it today? – (Today is) Tuesday.
What day is the 13th? – Monday.

5. **season** ['siːzn] — Jahreszeit; Saison
   in (the) **spring** [sprɪŋ] — im Frühling/Frühjahr
   summer ['sʌmə] — Sommer
   autumn ['ɔːtəm] — Herbst
   winter ['wɪntə] — Winter
   When? [wen] — Wann?

Spring is a very nice *season*.
May is a month *in (the) spring*.

July is a month *in (the) summer*.
October is a month *in (the) autumn*. [ɪn ðɪ 'ɔːtəm]
January is a month *in (the) winter*.
When's the football match? = *When* is ...?

6. **tomorrow** [tə'mɒrəʊ] — morgen
   next Monday [nekst] — (am) nächsten Montag

You must do your homework today, not *tomorrow*.
Can you come *tomorrow morning*? = ... morgen früh?

7. **How many?** [haʊ 'menɪ] — Wie viele?

How many brothers and sisters have you got?

Unit 5

1. **When's your birthday?** ['bɜːθdeɪ] — Wann hast du Geburtstag? Wann ist dein Geburtstag?
   on October 12th — am 12. Oktober

birthday
When's your birthday? It's in September.
Can I have a pet *for my birthday*?
= ... zum Geburtstag?
Can't we all go to London *on your birthday*?
= ... an deinem Geburtstag?

2. **party** (Pl.: **parties**) ['pɑːtɪ] — Party, Fest, Fete
   place [pleɪs] — Ort, Platz, Stelle
   so [səʊ] — darum, deshalb; also
   at the weekend [wiːk'end] — am Wochenende
   an [æn, ən] (vor Vokalen) — ein, eine
   (an) invitation to a party [ɪnvɪ'teɪʃn] — (eine) Einladung zu einer Feier

Kevin is from Dover. *So* he must be English.
Must you work *at the weekend*? – Only on Saturdays.

*a p*et — *an a*nimal
*a y*oung dog — *an o*ld dog

8 EG neu B1

113

| 5 A 3 | Let's go. [lets]
= **Let us** go.
(to) **take**, is **taking** [teɪk]
present ['preznt]
Why not ask Peter?

Why? [waɪ]
(an) **idea** [aɪ'dɪə]
She's crazy about Mike. [ə'baʊt]
crazy ['kreɪzɪ]
record ['rekɔːd]
record-player ['rekɔːdpleɪə] | Lass(t) uns gehen! Gehen wir (doch)!
(mit)nehmen; (hin)bringen, (weg)bringen

Geschenk
Warum fragen wir nicht Peter? Könnten wir nicht Peter fragen?
Warum? Weshalb?
(eine) Idee, (ein) Einfall
Sie ist ganz verrückt auf/ begeistert von Mike.
verrückt, wahnsinnig
Schallplatte
Plattenspieler | *Let's* go, Liz.

Hey, you can't *take* my cassette-recorder to the party. *Take* the old bike to the repair shop, please.

I've got a good *idea*. |

question words	
Why can't we go?	= Warum ...?
When's the party?	= Wann ...?
Where's Sandra?	= Wo ...?
Where's Sandra going?	= Wohin ...?
Where's Sandra from?	= Woher ...?
Who is Mr Hill?	= Wer ...?
What's she doing?	= Was ...?
What pets have you got?	= Was für ...?

5 A 4	**village** ['vɪlɪdʒ] **farm** [fɑːm]	Dorf Bauernhof, Farm	
5 A 5	**in the morning;** **in the afternoon;** **in the evening** **in the mornings;** **in the afternoons;** **in the evenings** **drink** [drɪŋk] **biscuit** ['bɪskɪt] **crisps** [krɪsps] a **bottle of** lemonade [ə 'bɒtl əv lemə'neɪd] (an) **orange** ['ɒrɪndʒ] **juice** [dʒuːs] a **packet** of ... ['pækɪt]	am Morgen/Vormittag; am Nachmittag; am Abend morgens/vormittags; nachmittags; abends Getränk Keks Kartoffelchips eine Flasche Limonade (eine) Apfelsine/Orange Saft ein Paket/Päckchen ...; eine Packung ...	Sandra's birthday party is *in the* [ðɪ] *afternoon*. Are you tired *in the mornings*? Can I have a *drink*, please?
5 A 6	(to) **prepare**, is **preparing** [prɪ'peə] **food** [fuːd] **sandwich** (Pl.: **sandwiches**) ['sænwɪdʒ] **cake** [keɪk]	vorbereiten, zubereiten Essen, Lebensmittel, Nahrung; Futter belegtes Butterbrot, Sandwich Kuchen	Sandra *is preparing* her party. She*'s preparing* food for five people. Can I have some *cake*? = ... etwas Kuchen? Let's make some *cakes*. = ... ein paar Kuchen.
5 A 7	**table** ['teɪbl] a **plate** of ... [pleɪt] a **tin** of ... [tɪn]	Tisch ein Teller (mit) ... eine Dose ..., eine Büchse ...	Mr Hill is sitting *at the table*. = ... am Tisch. There are two *plates on the table*.

Mengenangaben mit "of"

a bottle *of* lemonade = eine Flasche Limonade
a packet *of* biscuits = eine Packung Kekse
a box *of* pencils = eine Schachtel Bleistifte
plates *of* sandwiches = Teller mit belegten Broten
a small number *of* pupils = eine kleine Anzahl Schüler/von Schülern
lots *of* homework = eine Menge Hausaufgaben, viele Hausaufgaben

8	**this** book [ðɪs]	dieses Buch, das Buch (hier)
	these books [ði:z]	diese Bücher, die Bücher (hier)
	that book [ðæt]	das/dieses Buch (da), jenes Buch (dort)
	those books [ðəʊz]	die/diese Bücher (da), jene Bücher (dort)
	radio ['reɪdɪəʊ]	Radio; Rundfunk
	poster ['pəʊstə]	Poster, Plakat
	(an) **uncle** ['ʌŋkl]	(ein) Onkel
	(an) **aunt** [ɑ:nt]	(eine) Tante
	grandfather ['grænfɑ:ðə]	Großvater
	grandmother ['grænmʌðə]	Großmutter
9	**guest** [gest]	Gast
	(to) **fetch** [fetʃ]	holen; abholen
	him [hɪm]	ihm, ihn
	her [hɜ:, hə]	ihr, sie
	us [ʌs, əs]	uns
	them [ðem, ðəm]	ihnen, sie
	because [bɪ'kɒz]	weil
	See you soon.	Tschüs. Bis bald.
	soon [su:n]	bald
	Happy birthday (to you)!	Herzlichen Glückwunsch zum Geburtstag!
	happy ['hæpɪ]	glücklich, froh
	dear Sandra [dɪə]	liebe Sandra
T	**there** [ðeə]	da, dort; dahin, dorthin
	singer ['sɪŋə]	Sänger, Sängerin
	You're welcome. ['welkəm]	Bitte (sehr). Nichts zu danken. Gern geschehen.
	on the radio; on TV	im Radio; im Fernsehen
	programme ['prəʊgræm]	Sendung, Programm
◀ 3	the missing word ['mɪsɪŋ]	das fehlende Wort
6	**great** [greɪt]	großartig, prima, toll
	silly ['sɪlɪ]	albern, dumm, doof, blöd
9	**puzzle** ['pʌzl]	Rätsel
	letter ['letə]	Brief; Buchstabe
10	(to) **complete**, is completing [kəm'pli:t]	vervollständigen, ergänzen
	sentence ['sentəns]	Satz
12	(to) **write to** sb.	an jn. schreiben
	pen-friend ['- -]	Brieffreund, Brieffreundin
	photo ['fəʊtəʊ]	Foto, Aufnahme
	(to) **stop**, is **stopping** [stɒp]	aufhören; (an)halten, stoppen
	Yours, ... [jɔ:z]	dein(e) ...; Ihr(e) ...; euer/eure ... *(am Briefende)*
	rhyme [raɪm]	Reim, Vers
W	**board** [bɔ:d]	(Wand-)Tafel; Brett
	(to) **answer** ['ɑ:nsə]	antworten, beantworten

This is my pen. = *Das* ist ...

These are my books. = *Das* sind ...

What's *that*?
— It's a hamster.

Sandra has got a *radio*. She's listening to the *radio* now.

family	
parents:	grandparents:
mother/mum	grandmother
father/dad	grandfather
sister brother	aunt uncle

Where's Tom? Can you see *him*? We must help *him*.
Where's Tina? Can you hear *her*?

We can't help *them*
 because we're too busy.
See you soon/later/tomorrow/next week.

there	
da, dort	*dahin, dorthin*
Look, *there*'s Carol.	Why are you going *there*?

here	
hier	*(hier)her*
Here's my room.	Come *here*.

How many *letters* can you see?
— 1? Or 42?

Die verflixten sechs (SIE)	**Die verflixten vier (IHR)**
She's my friend.	*You*'re my friends.
They're my friends.	Why not help *her*?
You're my teacher, Mr Hill.	This is *her* bike.
I can see *her*.	That must be *their* dog.
I can see *them*.	
This is my bag. *It*'s new.	

p.57 **The time**

1 clock [klɒk] (Wand-, Stand-, Turm-)Uhr
watch (Pl.: watches) (Armband-)Uhr
[wɒtʃ]
quarter past ten Viertel nach zehn
['kwɔːtə pɑːst]
quarter to ten Viertel vor zehn
half past ten [hɑːf] halb elf (= 10.30)
(an) hour [ən ˈaʊə] (eine) Stunde
second ['sekənd] Sekunde

3 bus (Pl.: buses) [bʌs] Bus
train [treɪn] (Eisenbahn-)Zug
at 3 o'clock um 3 Uhr

Look at the *clock*. It's five o'clock.

⚠ *an* hour [ən ˈaʊə] – *a* house [ə ˈhaʊs]

When's the next *bus*? = Wann fährt der nächste Bus?
Let's take the *train* to London.

Unit 6

6 A 1 British ['brɪtɪʃ] britisch; Brite, Britin
(Great) Britain Großbritannien
['brɪtn]
(from ...) till [tɪl] (von ...) bis *(Zeitangabe)*
(to) wear [weə] (Kleidung) tragen, anhaben
(a) uniform (eine) Uniform
['juːnɪfɔːm]
lesson ['lesn]; Unterrichtsstunde;
lessons der Unterricht
(to) eat [iːt] essen
lunch [lʌntʃ] Mittagessen

6 A 2 (to) go to school zur/in die Schule gehen
(to) walk [wɔːk] (zu Fuß) gehen, laufen
(to) go by bike/train/ mit dem Fahrrad/Zug/
bus/car [baɪ] Bus/Auto fahren
(to) start (sth.) [stɑːt] (mit etwas) anfangen,
beginnen; starten
(to) go home nach Hause gehen
(to) finish (sth.) enden, (mit etwas) auf-
['fɪnɪʃ] hören; etwas beenden,
fertig machen
(to) get, is getting [get] bekommen, kriegen
after (school) ['ɑːftə] nach (der Schule)
(to) meet (sb.) [miːt] (jn.) treffen, sich (mit jm.)
treffen; jn. kennen lernen
club [klʌb] Verein, Club

6 A 3 child, children Kind, Kinder
[tʃaɪld, 'tʃɪldrən]
interesting ['ɪntrɪstɪŋ] interessant

James is from Scotland. He isn't English. But he's
British, of course.
Britain = England + Wales + Scotland
Summer is *from* June *till* September.
Dave *is wearing* his school *uniform*.
He's *carrying* a bag.

an [ən]	**a** [ə]
an uncle ['ʌŋkl]	*a* uniform ['juːnɪfɔːm]
an hour ['aʊə]	*a* unit ['juːnɪt]

In Germany lessons *start* at 8 o'clock.
Please *start* your homework soon.

Why must the party *finish* at 9 o'clock?
Let's *finish* the exercises and read the text again.

Kevin and Carol *get* lots of presents for their birthdays.

go — walk
Dave and Liz *are going* to school.
= They're on their way now.
Dave *is walking* and Liz *is going* by bike.
Can't we *go* to London? — Yes, but we can't *walk*
there, we must *go* by train.
⚠ Wie *geht* es dir? = How are you?

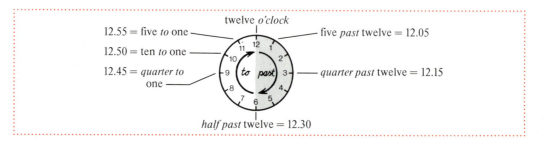

	model ['mɒdl]	Modell, Modell-
	table-tennis ['teɪbltenɪs]	Tischtennis
	stamp [stæmp]	(Brief-)Marke
	(to) **collect** [kə'lekt]	sammeln
	(to) **take photos/ pictures**	fotografieren, Fotos/ Bilder machen
5	hobby (Pl.: hobbies) ['hɒbɪ]	Hobby, Freizeitbeschäftigung
6	**(the) other** [ðɪ'ʌðə]	(der/die/das) andere
	coin [kɔɪn]	Münze
	(to) **play the guitar** [gɪ'tɑː]	Gitarre spielen
	(to) **learn** [lɜːn]	lernen
	piano [pɪ'ænəʊ]	Klavier
7	camera ['kæmrə]	Fotoapparat, Kamera
	(to) **use, is using** [juːz]	benutzen, gebrauchen, verwenden
8	(to) **get up, is getting up** [get'ʌp]	aufstehen
	breakfast ['brekfəst]	Frühstück
	(to) **drink** [drɪŋk]	trinken
	a **cup** of … [kʌp]	eine Tasse …
	tea [tiː]	Tee
	coffee ['kɒfɪ]	Kaffee
	(to) **leave** (a place), is **leaving** [liːv]	(von einem Ort) weggehen, abfahren; verlassen
	(to) **arrive,** is **arriving** [ə'raɪv]	ankommen, eintreffen
	(to) **do the housework** ['haʊswɜːk]	die Haus(halts)arbeit machen
10	**Don't laugh.** [daʊnt] = **Do not** laugh.	Lach(t) nicht! Lachen Sie nicht!
	sir [sɜː, sə]	Anrede, z. B. für den Lehrer/ einen Kunden im Laden
	ill [ɪl]	krank
	I've got a cold. [kəʊld]	Ich habe Schnupfen/eine Erkältung. Ich bin erkältet.
	That's all right. = **That's OK.**	Schon gut. Macht nichts. Nichts zu danken.
11	**lazy** ['leɪzɪ]	faul, träge
	(to) **run** (after sb.), is **running** [rʌn]	(hinter jm. her)rennen/ -laufen

Can you play *table-tennis*? — Yes, but we haven't got a *table-tennis* table.

> **What's your hobby?**
> I collect stamps/coins/photos/models.
> I play football/tennis/table-tennis.
> I play the guitar/the piano.
> I make models/cakes.
> I read books/take photos.

Some pupils go to the stamp club, *other* pupils go to the photo club.
Two girls play football, *the others* play table-tennis.

Kevin can't play the guitar or *the piano*.

Can I have your calculator? — Sorry, I*'m using* it.

Every morning Mr Hill *gets up* at 6.30.
You can't sit here. Please *get up*.
Mr Hill eats toast *for breakfast* … = … zum Frühstück …
… and *drinks a cup of tea.*

> **home**
> (to) go *home* = nach Hause gehen
> (to) arrive/come *home* = nach Hause kommen
> (to) leave *home* = von zu Hause weggehen

⚠ Sie macht ihre Hausaufgaben.
= She*'s doing her homework.*

Kevin (to Mr Hill): Can I open the window, *sir*?
Mr Singh (to Mr Dean): Can I help you, *sir*?
Sandra is *ill*, so she can't go to school.
Sandra *has got a cold*. Lots of other pupils in her class *have got colds,* too.
Sorry, I'm late. — *That's all right.*
Thanks for your help. — *That's OK.*

> „machen"
>
> (to) *make* = herstellen, (zusammen)bauen, zubereiten
>   Let's *make* a table/a nice present/a model car/the breakfast/sandwiches/a cake/a cup of coffee.
>   *Make* questions/sentences. = Bilde(t) Fragen!
>
> (to) *do* = tun, verrichten, erledigen
>   You must *do* your homework/the housework/the repairs.
>   Who can *do* the next sentence/exercise?
>   What *are* you *doing*? = Was machst du?
>
> ⚠ Fotos *machen* = (to) take photos

	ball [bɔːl]	Ball
	grass [grɑːs]	Gras
	another dog [əˈnʌðə]	ein anderer Hund; noch ein Hund
	café [ˈkæfeɪ]	Café; kleines Restaurant
	(to) **know** [nəʊ]	kennen; wissen
	still [stɪl]	trotzdem, dennoch
6 Ex 1	My watch is wrong/right.	Meine Uhr geht falsch/richtig.
4	(to) draw [drɔː]	zeichnen
11	Odd man out! [ˈɒd mæn ˈaʊt]	Welches Wort passt hier nicht?
6 Ww	(an) **exercise book** [ˈeksəsaɪz bʊk]	(ein) Heft, Schulheft
	(to) **shut, is shutting** [ʃʌt]	schließen, zumachen
	part [pɑːt]	Rolle (eines Schauspielers)

○ **Extra Reading**

job [dʒɒb]	Beruf, Arbeit
report (about) [rɪˈpɔːt]	Bericht (über)
disc jockey (DJ) [ˈdɪsk dʒɒkɪ, ˈdiːdʒeɪ]	Diskjockey
(to) think [θɪŋk]	meinen, finden
(to) tell sb. (about sth.) [tel]	jm. (über etwas) berichten, jm. (von etwas) erzählen

I can't write with this pen. Can I have *another* pen, please?

Of course I *know* Liz. We go to school together.
Have you *still* got a cold? — Yes, but you can *still* play with me.

> **rhyme words**
> know—no, hour—our, buy—Bye.—by, hear—here, right—write, sea—see, their—there, too—two, wear—where

Write the answers in your *exercise books*, please.

Open your books at page 67. Now *shut* them again, please.

PS [ˈpiːˈes]	PS (am Briefende)
studio [ˈstjuːdɪəʊ]	Studio
so [səʊ]	so
news [njuːz]	Nachrichten
work [wɜːk]	Arbeit
(to) make jokes [dʒəʊks]	Witze machen

Unit 7

7 A 1	magician [məˈdʒɪʃn]	Zauberer	
	Dr = Doctor [ˈdɒktə]	Dr. = Doktor	
	(to) **live, is living** [lɪv]	wohnen, leben	
	the name **of** the street [ɒv, əv]	der Name (von) der Straße	
	What colour is/are…?	Welche Farbe hat/haben…?	
	different (from) [ˈdɪfrənt]	verschieden, unterschiedlich; anders (als)	
7 A 2	downstairs [daʊnˈsteəz]	unten (im Haus); nach unten, (die Treppe) hinunter/herunter	
	upstairs [ʌpˈsteəz]	oben (im Haus); nach oben, (die Treppe) hinauf/herauf	
	stairs [steəz]	Treppe(nstufen)	
	green [griːn]	grün	
	(a book) **about** (cars)	(ein Buch) über (Autos)	
	magic [ˈmædʒɪk]	Zauberkunst, Magie	
	(to) do magic	zaubern	
	library (Pl.: libraries) [ˈlaɪbrərɪ]	Bibliothek, Bücherei	
	desk [desk]	Schreibtisch, Schülertisch	
	shelf (Pl.: shelves) [ʃelf, ʃelvz]	Bord, (Regal-)Brett; Regal	
	next to the library [ˈnekstə]	neben der Bibliothek	
	living-room [ˈlɪvɪŋrʊm]	Wohnzimmer	
	brown [braʊn]	braun	

Sorry I can't help you. I'm not a *magician*.
Sandra is ill. So *Dr* Jones must come.
The Deans *live* in Hatfield. I *live* in Frankfurt.

My room is *upstairs*, but my sister's room is *downstairs*.

Take the books *upstairs*, please. But come *downstairs* again.

> **Der Genitiv mit "'s" und "of"**
>
> Für Personen: **'s**
>   Dave**'s** book = Daves Buch
>   my mother**'s** bike = das Fahrrad meiner Mutter
>
> Für Sachen: **of**
>   the colour **of** the room = die Farbe des Zimmers
>   the name **of** the street = der Name (von) der Straße
>   Aber: one **of** the boys = einer der Jungen
>
> ⚠ Sandra has got a photo **of** Dave.
>   = … von Dave.
>   And she has got a letter **from** Dave, too.
>   = … von Dave.

wall [wɔ:l]	Wand; Mauer	
floor [flɔ:]	Fußboden	
ceiling ['si:lɪŋ]	Zimmerdecke	
between [bɪ'twi:n]	zwischen	
blue [blu:]	blau	
bedroom ['bedrʊm]	Schlafzimmer	
bed [bed]	Bett	

between Carol and Tina

▲ 3

grey [greɪ]	grau
kitchen ['kɪtʃɪn]	Küche
(to) **cook** [kʊk]	kochen, zubereiten
meal [mi:l]	Mahlzeit, Essen
over ['əʊvə]	über
under ['ʌndə]	unter
dining-room ['daɪnɪŋrʊm]	Esszimmer
orange ['ɒrɪndʒ]	orange(farben)
chair [tʃeə]	Stuhl
cupboard ['kʌbəd]	Schrank
red [red]	rot
bathroom ['bɑ:θrʊm]	Bad(ezimmer)
yellow ['jeləʊ]	gelb
lamp [læmp]	Lampe
inside (the house) [ɪn'saɪd]	innen/drinnen (im Haus); nach drinnen
outside (the house) [aʊt'saɪd]	draußen (vor dem Haus); nach draußen
ladder ['lædə]	Leiter

Kevin is *in bed* because he's ill.
Blacky is sitting *on the bed*.

My father *cooks* lunch on Sundays.
⚠ Kaffee/Tee *kochen* = (to) *make* coffee/tea

over the table   *over* the wall   *under* the car

> **colours**
> white, grey, black, yellow, green, blue, orange, red, brown
> ⚠ My room **is** three different colours.
> Mein Zimmer **hat** drei verschiedene Farben.

It's raining. Let's wait *inside* (the house).
— Yes, let's go *inside* (the house).
All the other children are playing *outside*. Why can't we go *outside*, too?

▲ 4

(to) share sth. (with sb.), is sharing [ʃeə]	(sich) etwas (mit jm.) teilen, etwas gemeinsam benutzen

▲ 5

job [dʒɒb]	Beruf, Arbeit, Job; Aufgabe
He's lucky. ['lʌkɪ]	Er hat Glück. Er ist gut dran.
(to) **go to work** [wɜ:k]	zur Arbeit gehen
always ['ɔ:lweɪz]	immer
usually ['ju:ʒʊəlɪ]	normalerweise, gewöhnlich
sometimes ['sʌmtaɪmz]	manchmal
often ['ɒfn, 'ɒftən]	oft
never ['nevə]	nie, niemals

What's Mr Hill's *job*? — He's a teacher.
Mr Hill does *jobs* at home at the weekend.
You're *lucky*, Sandra. Today must be your *lucky* day.
⚠ Er ist *glücklich/froh*. = He's *happy*.

Tom *usually* goes to school by bus.
He *sometimes* leaves very late, ...

... and so he *often* runs to the bus.
But he's *never* late.

▲ 6

comic ['kɒmɪk]	Comicheft

▲ 7

at the moment ['məʊmənt]	im Moment, im Augenblick; zurzeit

▲ 9

you	*hier:* man
(to) tidy up, he/she tidies up [taɪdɪ'ʌp]	aufräumen
(to) wash the dishes ['wɒʃ ðə 'dɪʃɪz]	(das Geschirr) spülen, abwaschen
(to) **wash**, he/she **washes** [wɒʃ]	waschen, sich waschen
(to) dry the dishes, he/she dries [draɪ]	(das Geschirr) abtrocknen

> 1. He's ti**dy**ing up now. | Vor dem -y steht
>   He often ti**die**s up. | ein Konsonant.
>
>   Ebenso: is drying — dries
>   is carrying — carries
>   is flying   — flies
>
> 2. She's st**ay**ing at home today. | Vor dem -y steht
>   She often st**ay**s at home. | ein Vokal.
>
>   Ebenso: is playing — plays
>   is buying — buys
>   is saying   — says

> **work—school** (ohne "the")
> (to) go *to work*/(to) be *at work*/(to) come home *from work/after work*
> (to) go *to school*/(to) be *at school*/(to) come home *from school/after school*

7 A 10	(to) **stay** [steɪ]	bleiben	
	(an) office [ˈɒfɪs]	(ein) Büro	
	husband [ˈhʌzbənd]	(Ehe-)Mann	
	mechanic [mɪˈkænɪk]	Mechaniker, Mechanikerin	
	when ... [wen]	wenn ...	

I don't know that man. Is he Mrs King's *husband*?
Of course a girl can be a *mechanic*. Why not?
You can't play outside *when* it's raining.
When Mr Hill comes home, he makes a cup of tea.
Sandra *thinks* Mike Walker is great.

7 A 11   (to) **think** [θɪŋk]   meinen, glauben, denken
He **doesn't** tidy up.   Er räumt nicht auf.
[ˈdʌznt] = He **does
not** tidy up.

7 T   **wife** (Pl.: **wives**)   (Ehe-)Frau
[waɪf, waɪvz]
(to) **argue** (about sth.),   sich (über/wegen etwas)
is arguing [ˈɑːgjuː]   streiten, zanken
night [naɪt]   Nacht, (später) Abend
behind [bɪˈhaɪnd]   hinter
furniture [ˈfɜːnɪtʃə]   Möbel
through [θruː]   durch, hindurch
(to) **like** [laɪk]   mögen, gern haben
I don't think so.   Das finde/glaube ich nicht.
I think so.   Ich glaube (ja).
(to) **agree** (with sb.)   (mit jm.) übereinstimmen/
[əˈgriː]   gleicher Meinung sein

Who is that woman? Isn't she Mr Connor's *wife*?
— Yes, that's Mrs Connor.

 behind the wall

⚠ This *furniture* **is** new. *(Kein Plural!)*

zustimmen	ablehnen, widersprechen
OK. All right. Yes.	I don't agree (with you).
Yes, that's right.	No, I think that's wrong.
That's a good idea.	I think it's a terrible idea.
I think so, too.	I don't think so.

7 Ex 4   (to) **correct** [kəˈrekt]   berichtigen, verbessern,
korrigieren
8   (to) **hate** [heɪt]   hassen, gar nicht mögen

7 Ww   (to) **understand**   verstehen, begreifen
[ʌndəˈstænd]
loud(er) [ˈlaʊdə]   laut(er)

I don't *understand* this sentence. What's it in German?

p.81   **British money**

money [ˈmʌnɪ]	Geld	
note [nəʊt]	(Geld-)Schein, Banknote	
£1 =a/one **pound**	ein Pfund *(britische*	
[paʊnd]	*Währung)*	
10**p** [piː]	zehn Pence	
= 10 **pence** [pens]		
cheap [tʃiːp]	billig	
expensive [ɪkˈspensɪv]	teuer	
How much is/are ...?	Was kostet/kosten ...?	
How much?	Wie viel?	
[haʊ ˈmʌtʃ]		

pound—**pounds** = **Pfund**
There are 100 pence in a *pound*.
£1   = one *pound*   (= ein Pfund)
£2   = two *pounds*   (= zwei Pfund)
£2.50 = two (*pounds*) fifty (= zwei Pfund fünfzig)
⚠ Punkt zwischen "pound" und "pence".
£ steht immer vor der Zahl.

They've got a *cheap* old flat, but an *expensive* new car.

How much is this record? — It*'s* £4.50. But those records *are* only £3.

How much (+ Singular)?
How much money has she got?
How much food can you eat?
How many (+ Plural)?
How many people are there?
How many biscuits can you eat?

Unit 8

8 A 1   pocket-money   Taschengeld
pocket [ˈpɒkɪt]   Tasche (im Mantel usw.)

8 A 2   (to) **ask** sb. **for** sth.   jn. um etwas bitten

8 A 3   (to) **save**, is **saving**   sparen
[seɪv]
50p a week   50 Pence pro Woche/
wöchentlich

Dave *is saving* his pocket-money for a new bike.

8 A 4   sweets [swiːts]   Süßigkeiten, Bonbons

5	(an) interview ['ɪntəvju:]	(ein) Interview	
	free time ['fri: 'taɪm]	Freizeit, freie Zeit	What do you do in your *free time*?
	about	ungefähr, etwa	
	sport [spɔ:t]	Sport, Sportart	
	(to) **practise**, is practising ['præktɪs]	üben, trainieren	Martin *practises* the guitar every day. The children *are practising* for the football match.
	music ['mju:zɪk]	Musik	
7	youth club ['ju:θ klʌb]	Jugendklub, Jugendzentrum	What do you do at your *youth club*? — We play games, listen to music and talk.
10	(shop) assistant [ə'sɪstənt]	Verkäufer, Verkäuferin	**What's his/her job?** He's/She's *a* teacher/*a* mechanic/*a* shop assistant. He/She works in an office. He/She doesn't work. = Er/Sie ist nicht berufstätig.
	(to) **sell** [sel]	verkaufen	
	Anything else? ['enɪθɪŋ 'els]	Sonst noch etwas?	
	I'm just looking. [dʒʌst]	Ich sehe mich nur um. *(im Geschäft)*	
T	sofa ['səʊfə]	Sofa	
	What is it? [wɒt 'ɪz ɪt]	Was ist denn (los)?	
	... **that** ... [ðæt, ðət]	..., dass ...	Tom says *(that)* he's never late.
	broken ['brəʊkən]	kaputt; zer-, gebrochen	
	(to) **spend** money (**on** sth.) [spend]	Geld ausgeben (für etwas)	Do you *spend* your pocket-money *on* sweets?
	(64203.) Mrs Carter here.	*(am Telefon:)* Hier Carter. (Frau) Carter am Apparat.	What's your telephone number? — 80285.
	0 [əʊ]	null *(in Telefonnummern)*	
	(to) **(tele)phone** sb.	jn. anrufen	Liz is on the phone. She *'s phoning* Sandra.
	about	wegen	
	stereo ['steriəʊ]	Stereo, Stereo-	**about**
	this morning/afternoon/evening	heute Morgen/Nachmittag/ Abend	I'm phoning *about* the party. = ... wegen ... a book *about* pop music = ... über ... *about* 3 hours = ungefähr ... crazy *about* sweets = verrückt auf ...
	road [rəʊd]	(Land-)Straße	
	(to) **give**, is **giving** [gɪv]	geben; schenken	
2	dialogue ['daɪəlɒg]	Dialog	
5	**Sorry?**	Wie bitte?	
9	**I'd like** ... [aɪd 'laɪk] = **I would like** ... [aɪ wəd 'laɪk]	Ich hätte/möchte gern ...	*I'd like* a C 60 cassette, please. *I'd like* some biscuits, please.
14	..., **you know.** [nəʊ]	weißt du, nämlich	Kevin isn't at school today. He's ill, *you know*.
15	**group** [gru:p]	Gruppe	There's a *group* of English pupils at our school.
	capital (letter) ['kæpɪtl]	Großbuchstabe	
w	(to) **mean** [mi:n]	bedeuten	What *does* the second word in line 14 *mean*? the sentence "It's my turn" ⚠ *Niemals:* What means ...?
	(to) **spell** [spel]	buchstabieren, schreiben	
	(to) **pronounce**, is **pronouncing** [prə'naʊns]	(Wort usw.) aussprechen	Don't *pronounce* the "p" in cupboard.

○ **Song**

	my Bonnie ['bɒnɪ]	meine Geliebte, mein Schatz	**this**
	... *is over the ocean* ['əʊvə ðɪ 'əʊʃn]	... ist über den Ozean gefahren	this week = diese Woche this year = dieses Jahr this morning = heute Morgen this afternoon = heute Nachmittag this evening/tonight = heute Abend
	(to) bring back [brɪŋ 'bæk]	zurückbringen	

Extra Reading

(to) hope [həʊp]		hoffen
strange [streɪndʒ]		seltsam, ausgefallen
plant [plɑ:nt]		Pflanze
rubber plant ['rʌbə plɑ:nt]		Gummibaum
water ['wɔ:tə]		Wasser
three metres long ['mi:təz]		drei Meter lang
(to) bring [brɪŋ]		(mit)bringen
boa constrictor ['bəʊə kənstrɪktə]		Boa constrictor (Riesenschlange)
before [bɪ'fɔ:]		bevor, ehe

Extra Unit – Unit 9

9 A 1

Excuse me, … [ɪk'skju:z mi:]	Entschuldigen Sie, …
hospital ['hɒspɪtl]	Krankenhaus
hotel [həʊ'tel]	Hotel
station ['steɪʃn]	Bahnhof
post office ['pəʊst ˌɒfɪs]	Post(amt)
church (Pl.: churches) [tʃɜ:tʃ]	Kirche
police station [pə'li:s steɪʃn]	Polizeiwache, Polizeirevier
cinema ['sɪnəmə]	Kino
bank [bæŋk]	Bank, Sparkasse
Can you tell me the way to the hospital? [tel]	Können Sie mir sagen, wie ich zum Krankenhaus komme?
along… [ə'lɒŋ]	…entlang, hinunter
(to) turn left/right [tɜ:n left, raɪt]	(nach) links/rechts abbiegen
into ['ɪntʊ, 'ɪntə]	in … (hinein)
on the left; on the right	links, auf der linken Seite; rechts, auf der rechten Seite

9 A 2

(to) tell sb. about sth.	jm. von etwas erzählen
history ['hɪstrɪ]	Geschichte, Vergangenheit
(to) visit ['vɪzɪt]	besuchen, besichtigen
popular ['pɒpjʊlə]	beliebt
tourist ['tʊərɪst]	Tourist, Urlauber
beautiful ['bju:tɪfl]	schön
huge [hju:dʒ]	sehr groß, riesig
town centre ['taʊn ˌsentə]	Stadtmitte, Stadtzentrum
boring ['bɔ:rɪŋ]	langweilig
square [skweə]	Platz (in einer Stadt)
fountain ['faʊntɪn]	Springbrunnen
at least [ət 'li:st]	mindestens, zumindest
pedestrian precinct [pɪ'destrɪən 'pri:sɪŋkt]	Fußgängerzone
bad [bæd]	schlecht
super ['su:pə]	fantastisch, toll; Super-
modern ['mɒdn]	modern
Love, … [lʌv]	Viele liebe Grüße von …
noisy ['nɔɪzɪ]	laut, von Lärm erfüllt

9 A 3

(an) island ['aɪlənd]	(eine) Insel
more than ['mɔ: ðən]	mehr als
120 kilometres ['kɪləmi:təz]	120 Kilometer
(to) go to the coast [kəʊst]	an die Küste/ans Meer fahren
(to) go/be on holiday ['hɒlɪdɪ]	in Urlaub fahren/sein
beach [bi:tʃ]	Strand
on the beach	am Strand
warm [wɔ:m]	warm

9 A 4

lake [leɪk]	(Binnen-)See
mountain ['maʊntɪn]	Berg
river ['rɪvə]	Fluss

9 A 5

(to) lie, is lying [laɪ]	liegen
postcard ['pəʊstkɑ:d]	Postkarte
souvenir [su:və'nɪə]	(Reise-)Andenken, Souvenir
(to) stay (at)	übernachten (in, auf)
guest house ['gest haʊs]	Pension, Gästehaus
bed and breakfast	Übernachtung mit Frühstück
youth hostel ['ju:θ hɒstl]	Jugendherberge
camp site ['kæmp saɪt]	Zeltplatz, Campingplatz

9 T

(to) see the sights [saɪts]	sich die Sehenswürdigkeiten ansehen
famous ['feɪməs]	berühmt
museum [mju:'zɪəm]	Museum
York [jɔ:k]	Stadt in Nordengland
for example [fər ɪg'zɑ:mpl]	zum Beispiel
the Minster ['mɪnstə]	Kathedrale von York
Chester ['tʃestə]	Stadt in Nordwestengland
Liverpool ['lɪvəpu:l]	Stadt in Nordwestengland
Buckingham Palace ['bʌkɪŋəm 'pæləs]	Londoner Wohnsitz der königlichen Familie
from the outside	von außen
(to) go in	hineingehen
the Queen [kwi:n]	die (britische) Königin
castle ['kɑ:sl]	Burg, Schloss
hill [hɪl]	Hügel, Berg
Caernarfon Castle [kə'nɑ:vn]	Burg in Wales
Wales [weɪlz]	Wales
Cornwall ['kɔ:nwəl]	Grafschaft im Südwesten Englands
Tintagel Castle [tɪn'tædʒl]	Burgruine in Cornwall
King Arthur [kɪŋ 'ɑ:θə]	König Artus
Loch Ness [lɒx, lɒk 'nes]	See in Nordschottland
Scotland ['skɒtlənd]	Schottland
monster ['mɒnstə]	Ungeheuer
water ['wɔ:tə]	Wasser
cold [kəʊld]	kalt
map [mæp]	(Land-)Karte

Alphabetical list of words

Intro = Introduction · 1 A 1 = Unit 1, Acquisition 1 · 2 T = Unit 2, Text · 3 Ex = Unit 3, Exercises ·
4 S = Unit 4, Summary · 5 Ww = Unit 5, Was sage ich, wenn …? · p. 47, 1 = Zusatzseite S. 47, Abschnitt 1
Die fett gedruckten Wörter gehören zum produktiven, die normal gedruckten zum rezeptiven Wortschatz.

A

a Intro — ein, eine
 50p a week 8 A 3 — 50 Pence pro Woche
about 7 A 2 — über
about 8 A 5; 8 T — ungefähr, etwa; wegen
across 4 A 10 — (quer) über, (quer) durch
activity Intro — Projekt, Beschäftigung
after 6 A 2 — nach
after 6 T — hinter … her
afternoon 1 Ex — Nachmittag
 Good afternoon. 1 Ex — Guten Tag! *(nachmittags)*
 in the afternoon(s) 5 A 5 — nachmittags
 this afternoon 8 T — heute Nachmittag
again 4 T — wieder; noch (ein)mal
(to) **agree** (with sb.) 7 T — (mit jm.) übereinstimmen/gleicher Meinung sein
all 4 A 1 — alle; alles
all right 2 Ex — gut, in Ordnung
 I'm all right. 2 Ex — Mir geht's gut.
 That's all right. 6 A 10 — Schon gut. Macht nichts. Nichts zu danken.
always 7 A 5 — immer
am Intro — bin
an 5 A 2 — ein, eine
and Intro — und
animal 4 A 7 — Tier
another 6 T — ein(e) anderer (-e, -es); noch ein(e)
answer 3 Ex — Antwort
(to) **answer** 5 Ww — antworten, beantworten
Anything else? 8 A 10 — Sonst noch etwas?
April p. 47, 1 — April
are 1 A 4 — bist, sind, seid
(to) **argue** (about sth.) 7 T — sich (über/wegen etwas) streiten, zanken
(to) **arrive** 6 A 8 — ankommen, eintreffen
(to) **ask: Ask** a partner. 1 A 2 — Frag(t) einen Partner/ eine Partnerin!
 Ask a question. 1 Ex — Stell(t) eine Frage!
(to) **ask** sb. **for** sth. 8 A 2 — jn. um etwas bitten
assistant: (shop) assistant 8 A 10 — Verkäufer, Verkäuferin
at: at Dave's/my house 2 A 5 — bei Dave/mir zu Hause
at home 2 A 5 — zu Hause
at school 1 A 5 — in der Schule
at the moment 7 A 2 — im Moment, im Augenblick; zur Zeit
at the weekend 5 A 2 — am Wochenende
at 3 o'clock p. 57, 3 — um 3 Uhr
August p. 47, 1 — August
aunt 5 A 8 — Tante
autumn p. 47, 5 — Herbst

B

bag 2 A 7 — Tasche, Beutel, Tüte
balcony 2 A 4 — Balkon
ball 6 T — Ball
(to) **bark** 4 A 8 — bellen
basket 4 A 3 — Korb
bathroom 7 A 3 — Bad(ezimmer)
(to) **be** 1 S — sein
 (to) be hungry 3 A 9 — Hunger haben, hungrig sein
 (to) **be late** 2 Ww — zu spät kommen
 (to) be lucky 7 A 5 — Glück haben
 (to) be sb.'s turn 4 A 6 — an der Reihe sein
because 5 A 9 — weil
bed 7 A 2 — Bett
 in bed 7 A 2 — im Bett
bedroom 7 A 2 — Schlafzimmer
behind 7 T — hinter
best 7 A 2 — bester, beste, bestes
between 7 A 2 — zwischen
big 2 A 4 — groß
bike 3 A 2 — Fahrrad, Rad
 by bike 6 A 2 — mit dem Fahrrad
 on a bike 3 T — mit dem Fahrrad
bird 4 A 8 — Vogel
biro 2 A 7 — Kugelschreiber, Kuli
birthday 5 A 1 — Geburtstag
 for sb.'s birthday 5 A 1 — zum Geburtstag
 Happy birthday (to you)! 5 A 9 — Herzlichen Glückwunsch zum Geburtstag!
 on your birthday 5 A 1 — an deinem Geburtstag
 When's your birthday? 5 A 1 — Wann hast du Geburtstag?
biscuit 5 A 5 — Keks
black 2 A 4 — schwarz
blue 7 A 2 — blau
board 5 Ww — (Wand-)Tafel; Brett
book 2 A 7 — Buch
bottle: a bottle of lemonade 5 A 5 — eine Flasche Limonade
box 4 A 3 — Kiste, Kasten; Schachtel

boy 1 A 6 — Junge
breakfast 6 A 8 — Frühstück
 for breakfast 6 A 8 — zum Frühstück
Britain: (Great) Britain 6 A 1 — Großbritannien
British 6 A 1 — britisch; Brite, Britin
broken 8 T — kaputt; zer-, gebrochen
brother 1 A 3 — Bruder
brown 7 A 2 — braun
budgie 4 A 3 — Wellensittich
bus p. 57, 3 — Bus
 by bus 6 A 2 — mit dem Bus
busy 3 Ex — beschäftigt
but 1 A 3 — aber
(to) **buy** 3 A 3 — kaufen
by: (to) **go by bike/bus/car/train** 6 A 2 — mit dem Rad/Bus/ Auto/Zug fahren
Bye. 1 Ex — Wiedersehen! Tschüs!

C

café 6 T — Café; kleines Restaurant
cage 4 A 3 — Käfig
cake 5 A 6 — Kuchen
calculator 2 A 7 — Taschenrechner
calendar p. 47, 1 — Kalender
camera 6 A 7 — Fotoapparat, Kamera
can 4 A 2 — können, dürfen
 Can I help you? 4 A 4 — Kann ich Ihnen/ dir behilflich sein?
 can't = cannot 4 A 9 — nicht können
capital (letter) 8 Ex — Großbuchstabe
car 2 A 4 — Auto, Wagen
 by car 6 A 2 — mit dem Auto
careful: Be careful, 4 A 7 — Sei(d) vorsichtig!
(to) **carry** 4 A 8 — tragen
cassette 3 A 3 — Cassette
cassette-recorder 3 A 3 — Cassettenrecorder
cat 2 A 4 — Katze
(to) **catch** 4 A 8 — fangen, erwischen
ceiling 7 A 2 — Zimmerdecke
chair 7 A 3 — Stuhl
cheap p. 81 — billig
child, children 6 A 3 — Kind, Kinder
class 1 A 1 — Klasse
(to) **clean** 3 A 7 — putzen, reinigen
clever 4 A 8 — klug, schlau; *hier:* geschickt
(to) **climb** 4 A 8 — klettern, steigen

123

clock p. 57, 1	(Wand-, Stand-, Turm-)Uhr	(to) draw 6 Ex	zeichnen		from Intro	von; aus
o'clock 3 A 1	... Uhr	dream 4 A 10	Traum		I'm from ... Intro	Ich bin/ komme aus ...
club 6 A 2	Verein, Club	drink 5 A 5	Getränk		Where are you from? 1 A 2	Wo kommst du her?
coffee 6 A 8	Kaffee	(to) drink 6 A 8	trinken		from ... till 6 A 1	von ... bis (Zeitangabe)
coin 6 A 6	Münze	(to) dry the dishes 7 A 9	(das Geschirr) abtrocknen		funny 4 A 7	lustig, komisch, witzig
cold: I've got a cold. 6 A 10	Ich habe Schnupfen/ eine Erkältung.				furniture 7 T	Möbel
(to) collect 6 A 3	sammeln	**E**				
colour 2 Ex	Farbe				**G**	
What colour is/ are ...? 7 A 1	Welche Farbe hat/ haben ...?	(to) eat 6 A 1	essen			
combination exercise 1 Ex	Kombinations- übung, Zuordnungs- übung	England Intro	England		game 2 A 7	Spiel
		English 1 A 1	englisch; Engländer, Engländerin; Englisch		garage 2 A 4	Garage
					garden 2 A 4	Garten
(to) come 3 A 10	kommen, mitkommen	in English 1 Ex	auf Englisch		German 1 A 5	deutsch; Deutscher, Deutsche; Deutsch
Come here. 5 T	Komm her.	evening 1 Ex	Abend			
comic 7 A 6	Comicheft	in the evening(s) 5 A 5	abends		Germany Intro	Deutschland
(to) complete 5 Ex	vervollständigen, ergänzen				(to) get 6 A 2	bekommen, kriegen
		this evening 8 T	heute Abend		(to) get up 6 A 8	aufstehen
(to) cook 7 A 3	kochen, zubereiten	every 4 A 5	jeder, jede, jedes		girl 1 A 6	Mädchen
(to) correct 7 Ex	berichtigen, verbes- sern, korrigieren	everything 4 A 10	alles		(to) give 8 T	geben; schenken
		exercise 1 Ex	Übung, Übungs- aufgabe		(to) go 3 A 10	gehen; fahren
crazy 5 A 3	verrückt, wahnsinnig				(to) go by bike/ bus/car/train 6 A 2	mit dem Rad/Bus/ Auto/Zug fahren
(to) be crazy about 5 A 3	ganz verrückt sein auf, begeistert sein von	exercise book 6 Ww	Heft, Schulheft			
crisps 5 A 5	Kartoffelchips	expensive p. 81	teuer		(to) go on 3 Ex	weitermachen
cup: a cup of ... 6 A 8	eine Tasse ...	(to) explain 4 Ww	erklären, erläutern		(to) go on Mum's bike 3 T	mit Muttis Rad fahren
cupboard 7 A 3	Schrank				good 1 A 1	gut
					Good afternoon. 1 Ex	Guten Tag! (nachmittags)
D		**F**			Good morning. 1 A 1	Guten Morgen! Guten Tag!
Dad, dad 2 A 5	Vati, Papa, Papi	family 2 A 1	Familie		Goodbye. 1 Ex	Auf Wiedersehen!
date p. 47, 4	Datum	fantastic 2 A 6	fantastisch, toll		grandfather 5 A 8	Großvater
What date is it (today)? p. 47, 4	Der Wievielte ist heute?	farm 5 A 4	Bauernhof, Farm		grandmother 5 A 8	Großmutter
		father 2 A 1	Vater			
day 4 A 5	Tag	favourite 4 A 7	Lieblings-		grandparents 5 A 8	Großeltern
dear 5 A 9	lieb	February p. 47, 1	Februar		grass 6 T	Gras
December p. 47, 1	Dezember				great 5 Ex	großartig, prima, toll
		(to) feed 4 A 5	füttern		green 7 A 2	grün
desk 7 A 2	Schülertisch, Schreib- tisch	felt-tip 2 A 7	Filzstift		grey 7 A 3	grau
		(to) fetch 5 A 9	holen; abholen		group 6 Ex	Gruppe
dialogue 8 Ex	Dialog	(to) fill in 1 Ex	einsetzen		guest 5 A 9	Gast
different (from) 7 A 1	verschieden, unterschiedlich; anders (als)	(to) find 2 Ex	finden		guitar: (to) play the guitar 6 A 6	Gitarre spielen
		(to) finish 6 A 2	enden, (mit etwas) aufhören; etwas be- enden, fertig machen			
dining-room 7 A 3	Esszimmer				**H**	
dishes: (to) wash/ dry the dishes 7 A 9	(das Geschirr) spülen, abwaschen/abtrock- nen	flat 2 A 4	Wohnung			
		floor 7 A 2	Fußboden		half past ten p. 57, 1	halb elf (= 10.30)
(to) do 3 A 4	tun, machen	(to) fly 4 A 8	fliegen		Hallo. Intro	Hallo! (Guten) Tag!
Don't laugh. 6 A 10	Lach(t) nicht.	food 5 A 5	Essen, Lebensmittel, Nahrung; Futter		hamster 4 A 2	Hamster
					happy 5 A 9	glücklich, froh
(to) do homework 3 A 5	die Hausaufgabe(n)/ Schularbeiten machen	football 3 A 11	Fußball		Happy birthday (to you)! 5 A 9	Herzlichen Glück- wunsch zum Geburtstag!
		for 1 Ww	für			
		for breakfast 6 A 8	zum Frühstück			
(to) do magic 7 A 2	zaubern	for sb.'s birthday 5 A 1	zum Geburtstag		has got 2 A 3	hat, besitzt
		form 1 Ex	Form		(to) hate 7 Ex	hassen, gar nicht mögen
(to) do the housework 6 A 8	die Haus(halts)arbeit machen	free time 8 A 5	Freizeit, freie Zeit			
		French 4 A 10	französisch; Franzose, Französin; Französisch		have got 2 A 2	haben, besitzen
dog 2 A 2	Hund				I've got a cold. 6 A 10	Ich habe einen Schnupfen/ eine Erkältung.
door 3 A 3	Tür					
downstairs 7 A 2	unten (im Haus); nach unten	Friday 4 A 6	Freitag			
		friend 1 A 9	Freund, Freundin			
Dr = Doctor 7 A 1	Dr. = Doktor				he 1 A 6	er

(to) **hear** 4 A 7	hören	**in the after-**	nachmittags	lesson; lessons 6 A 1	Unterrichtsstunde; der Unterricht
help 4 A 7	Hilfe	**noon(s)** 5 A 5		**let's** = **let us**	lass(t) uns
(to) **help** (sb. with sth.) 3 A 2	(jm. bei etwas) helfen	**in the evening(s)** 5 A 5	abends	5 A 3	
Can I help you? 4 A 4	Kann ich Ihnen/dir behilflich sein?	**in the morning(s)** 5 A 5	morgens	**letter** 5 Ex	Brief; Buchstabe
her 1 A 8; 5 A 9	ihr, ihre; ihr, sie	**in the picture** 4 Ex	auf dem Bild	**library** 7 A 2	Bibliothek, Bücherei
here Intro	hier	in (the) **spring**	im Frühling/	(to) **lift** 4 A 10	heben, hochheben
Come here. 5 T	Komm her.	p. 47, 5	Frühjahr	(to) **like** 7 T	mögen, gern haben
Here you are. 3 T	Hier bitte. Bitte sehr.	**in the street** 4 A 3	auf der Straße	I'd like ... = **I would like** ...	Ich hätte/möchte gern ...
(642031.) Mrs Carter here. 8 T	*(am Telefon:)* Hier Carter.	India 4 A 3	Indien	8 Ex	
hidden 4 Ex	versteckt, verborgen	**inside** (the house) 7 A 3	innen/drinnen (im Haus); nach drinnen	line 4 T	Zeile; Linie
him 5 A 9	ihm, ihn	**interesting** 6 A 3	interessant	(to) **listen to** sth./ sb. 3 A 7	sich etwas anhören; jm. zuhören, auf jn. hören
his 1 A 8	sein, seine	interview 8 A 5	Interview		
hobby 6 A 5	Hobby, Freizeit- beschäftigung	introduction Intro	Einführung, Einleitung	listening com- prehension 3 Ex	Hörverstehen
home 4 A 10	Heim, Zuhause	**invitation** (to a party) 5 A 2	Einladung (zu einer Feier)	little 3 T	klein, jung
at home 2 A 5	zu Hause, daheim	**is** Intro, 1 A 6	ist	(to) **live** 7 A 1	wohnen, leben
(to) go **home** 6 A 2	nach Hause gehen	**it** Intro; 3 A 2	es, (er, sie; ihn, sie)	lively 1 A 6	lebhaft
homework: (to) **do your homework** 3 A 5	die Hausaufgabe(n)/ Schularbeiten machen	**its** 2 S	sein, seine; ihr, ihre	living-room 7 A 2	Wohnzimmer
				long 1 Ex	lang
		J		(to) **look** 4 A 3	sehen, schauen, gucken
hour p. 57, 1	Stunde	**January:** in **January** p. 47, 1	im Januar	I'm just looking. 8 A 10	Ich sehe mich nur um. *(im Geschäft)*
house 2 A 4	Haus	Japanese 4 A 10	japanisch; Japaner, Japanerin; Japanisch	(to) **look at** 4 A 3	(sich) etwas anschauen
at Dave's/my house 2 A 5	bei Dave/mir zu Hause	**job** 7 A 5	Beruf, Arbeit, Job; Aufgabe	lots (of ...) 2 T	viele, viel, eine Menge
housework: (to) **do the housework** 6 A 8	die Haus(halts)arbeit machen	juice 5 A 5	Saft	loud(er) 7 Ww	laut(er)
		June p. 47, 1	Juni	lucky: He's lucky. 7 A 5	Er hat Glück. Er ist gut dran.
how: How are you? 2 Ex	Wie geht's (dir/Ihnen)?	**July** p. 47, 1	Juli	lunch 6 A 1	Mittagessen
How many? p. 47, 7	Wie viele?	**just:** I'm just looking. 8 A 10	Ich sehe mich nur um. *(im Geschäft)*	**M**	
How much? p. 81	Wie viel?			magazine 2 A 7	Zeitschrift, Illustrierte
How much is/ are ...? p. 81	Was kostet/ kosten ...?	**K**		magic 7 A 2	Zauberkunst, Magie
How old are you? 1 A 2	Wie alt bist du?	**kit:** a repair kit 3 T	(eine Tasche mit) Flickzeug	(to) do magic 7 A 2	zaubern
hungry: (to) be hungry 3 A 9	Hunger haben, hungrig sein	**kitchen** 7 A 3	Küche	magician 7 A 1	Zauberer
(to) **hurry up** 3 A 1	sich beeilen	(to) **know** 6 T	kennen; wissen	(to) **make** p. 47, 1	machen, bauen
husband 7 A 10	(Ehe-)Mann	**you know** 8 Ex	weißt du, nämlich	man, men 3 A 11	Mann, Männer
				many: How many? p. 47, 7	Wie viele?
I		**L**		**March** p. 47, 1	März
I Intro	ich	**ladder** 7 A 3	Leiter	match 3 A 5	Spiel, Wettkampf, Match
I'd like ... = **I would like** ... 8 Ex	Ich hätte/möchte gern ...	lamp 7 A 3	Lampe	**may** 4 A 4	dürfen
		late: Sorry I'm late. 2 Ww	Entschuldigen Sie, dass ich zu spät komme.	May p. 47, 1	Mai
I'm from ... Intro	Ich bin/komme aus ...			me 3 A 2	mir, mich
I'm OK/all right. 2 Ex	Mir geht's gut.	later 3 T	später	meal 7 A 3	Mahlzeit, Essen
idea 5 A 3	Idee, Einfall	(to) **laugh** 4 A 7	lachen	(to) **mean** 8 Ww	bedeuten
ill 6 A 10	krank	lazy 6 T	faul, träge	mechanic 7 A 10	Mechaniker, Mechanikerin
in Intro	in	(to) **learn** 6 A 6	lernen	(to) **meet** (sb.) 6 A 2	(jn.) treffen, sich (mit jm.) treffen; jn. kennen lernen
in a minute 3 A 10	gleich, sofort	(to) **leave** (a place) 6 A 8	(von einem Ort) weggehen, abfahren; verlassen		
in bed 7 A 2	im Bett			mile: It's ten miles to .... 3 T	Es sind zehn Meilen bis (nach/zu) ....
in English 1 Ex	auf Englisch	lemonade: a **bottle of** lemonade 5 A 5	eine Flasche Limonade	minute 3 A 10	Minute
in **January** p. 47, 1	im Januar			in a minute 3 A 10	gleich, sofort

125

Miss ... 1 Ex	Fräulein/Frau ...	of: the name of the street 7 A 1	der Name (von) der Straße	phone = telephone 3 A 9	Telefon
missing 5 Ex	fehlend	of course 1 A 9	natürlich, selbstverständlich	(to) be on the (tele)phone 3 A 9	am Telefon sein, gerade telefonieren
model 6 A 3	Modell, Modell-	office 7 A 10	Büro	(to) (tele)phone sb. 8 T	jn. anrufen
moment: at the moment 7 A 7	im Moment, im Augenblick; zurzeit	often 7 A 5	oft	photo 5 Ex	Foto, Aufnahme
Monday: on Monday(s) 4 A 6	montags, am Montag	OK = okay 2 Ex	gut, in Ordnung	(to) take photos 6 A 3	fotografieren, Fotos/ Bilder machen
money p. 81	Geld	I'm OK. 2 Ex	Mir geht's gut.	piano 6 A 6	Klavier
month p. 47, 1	Monat	old: How old are you? 1 A 2	Wie alt bist du?	picture 4 Ex	Bild; Aufnahme, Foto
morning 1 A 1	Morgen, Vormittag	on 2 A 4	auf; an	in the picture 4 Ex	auf dem Bild
Good morning. 1 A 1	Guten Morgen! Guten Tag!	I'm on my way (to ...). 3 A 10	Ich bin auf dem Weg/ unterwegs (nach/ zu ...).	(to) take pictures 6 A 3	fotografieren, Fotos/ Bilder machen
in the morning(s) 5 A 5	morgens, vormittags	on a bike 3 T	mit dem Fahrrad	pity: It's a pity. 2 T	Das ist schade.
this morning 8 T	heute Morgen	on Monday(s) 4 A 6	montags, am Montag	place 5 A 2	Ort, Platz, Stelle
tomorrow morning p. 47, 6	morgen früh	on October 12th 5 A 1	am 12. Oktober	plate: a plate of ... 3 A 3	ein Teller (mit) ...
mother 2 A 1	Mutter	on the phone 3 A 9	am Telefon	(to) play 3 A 3	spielen
mouse, mice 4 A 3	Maus, Mäuse	on the radio 5 T	im Radio	please 3 A 1	bitte
Mr ... 1 A 1	Herr ...	on TV 5 T	im Fernsehen	pocket 8 A 1	Tasche (im Mantel usw.)
Mrs ... 2 A 1	Frau ...	on your birthday 5 A 1	an deinem Geburtstag	pocket-money 8 A 1	Taschengeld
much: How much? p. 81	Wie viel?	only 4 A 7	nur	poor 4 A 10	arm
How much is/ are ...? p. 81	Was kostet/ kosten ...?	(to) open 4 A 7	öffnen, aufmachen	poster 5 A 8	Poster, Plakat
Mum, mum 2 A 5	Mutti, Mama, Mami	or 2 A 2	oder	pound p. 81	ein Pfund (britische Währung)
music 8 A 5	Musik	orange 5 A 5; 7 A 3	Apfelsine, Orange; orange(farben)	(to) practise 8 A 5	üben, trainieren
must 4 A 5	müssen	(the) other 6 A 6	(der/die/das) andere	(to) prepare 5 A 6	vorbereiten, zubereiten
my Intro	mein, meine	our 2 A 6	unser, unsere	present 5 A 3	Geschenk
		outside (the house) 7 A 3	draußen (vor dem Haus); nach draußen	problem 3 A 2	Problem, Schwierigkeit
N		over 7 A 3	über	programme 5 T	Sendung, Programm
name: What's your name? 1 A 3	Wie ist dein Name? Wie heißt du?	owner 4 A 3	Besitzer, Besitzerin	(to) pronounce 8 Ww	aussprechen
near Intro	in der Nähe von, nahe (bei)	**P**		puncture 3 A 2	Reifenpanne
never 7 A 5	nie, niemals			pupil 1 A 5	Schüler, Schülerin
new Intro	neu	p = pence p. 81	Pence	puzzle 5 Ex	Rätsel
newspaper 2 A 7	Zeitung	packet: a packet of ... 5 A 5	ein Paket/Päckchen ...; eine Packung ...		
next Monday p. 47, 6	(am) nächsten Montag	page 3 Ww	Seite (im Buch)	**Q**	
next to sb./sth. 7 A 2	neben jm./ etwas	(to) paint 3 A 3	(an)streichen; malen	quarter past/to ten p. 57, 1	Viertel nach/vor zehn
nice 1 A 6	nett, schön, hübsch	paper 2 A 7	Zeitung	question: Ask a question. 1 Ex	Stell(t) eine Frage!
night 7 T	Nacht, (später) Abend	parents 2 A 1	Eltern	quiet 1 A 6	still, ruhig, leise
no 1 A 3; 3 A 2	nein; kein, keine	park 3 T	Park	quiz 2 A 2	Quiz, Frage-und- Antwort-Spiel
not 1 A 3	nicht	part 6 Ww	Rolle (eines Schauspielers)		
note p. 81	(Geld-)Schein, Banknote	partner: Ask a partner. 1 A 2	Frag(t) einen Partner/ eine Partnerin!	**R**	
nothing 3 A 11	nichts	party 5 A 2	Party, Fest, Fete		
November p. 47, 1	November	past: half past ten p. 57, 1	halb elf (= 10.30)	rabbit 1 A 6	Kaninchen
now 3 A 2	jetzt, nun	pen 2 A 7	Füller; Stift (außer Bleistift)	radio 5 A 8	Radio; Rundfunk
number 2 A 7	Zahl, Nummer; Anzahl	pence p. 81	Pence	on the radio 5 T	im Radio
		pencil 2 A 7	Bleistift	(to) rain 4 T	regnen
O		pencil-case 2 A 7	Federtasche, Federmäppchen	(to) read 3 A 7	lesen; vorlesen
o'clock 3 A 1	... Uhr	pen-friend 5 Ex	Brieffreund, Brieffreundin	record 5 A 3	Schallplatte
October p. 47, 1	Oktober	people 4 A 1	Leute, Menschen	record-player 5 A 3	Plattenspieler
Odd man out! 6 Ex	Welches Wort passt hier nicht?	pet 2 T	Haustier, Tier	red 7 A 3	rot
		pet shop 4 A 3	Tierhandlung	(to) repair 3 A 2	reparieren

repair kit: a repair kit 3 T	(eine Tasche mit) Flickzeug	(to) sit 3 A 11	sitzen	
repair shop 3 A 7	Reparaturwerkstatt für Fahrräder	(to) sit down 3 A 11	sich setzen	
		(to) sleep 3 A 11	schlafen	
rhyme 5 Ex	Reim, Vers	small 1 A 6	klein	
right 1 A 4	richtig	so 5 A 2	darum, deshalb; also	
all right 2 Ex	gut, in Ordnung	I don't think so. 7 T	Das glaube/finde ich nicht.	
My watch is right. 6 Ex	Meine Uhr geht richtig.	I think so. 7 T	Ich glaube (ja).	
That's right. 1 A 4	Das ist richtig. Stimmt!	sofa 8 T	Sofa	
road 8 T	(Land-)Straße	some 4 A 3	einige, ein paar; etwas	
role-play 1 Ex	Rollenspiel	sometimes 7 A 5	manchmal	
room 3 A 5	Zimmer, Raum	song Intro	Lied	
round Intro	Kanon	soon 5 A 9	bald	
rubber 2 A 7	Radiergummi; Gummi	sorry: (I'm) sorry. 2 Ww	Entschuldigung! Tut mir Leid!	
ruler 2 A 7	Lineal	Sorry? 8 Ex	Wie bitte?	
(to) run (after sb.) 6 T	(hinter jm. her)rennen/laufen	Sorry I'm late. 2 Ww	Entschuldigen Sie, dass ich zu spät komme.	
		sound 1 Ex	Laut, Ton; Klang	
S		(to) speak (to sb.) 4 A 10	(mit jm.) sprechen	
same: the same 1 A 9	der-, die-, dasselbe; dieselben	(to) spell 8 Ww	buchstabieren, schreiben	
sandwich 5 A 6	belegtes Butterbrot, Sandwich	(to) spend money (on sth.) 8 T	Geld ausgeben (für etwas)	
Saturday 3 A 1	Samstag, Sonnabend	sport 8 A 5	Sport, Sportart	
(to) save 8 A 3	sparen	spring: in (the) spring p. 47, 5	im Frühling/Frühjahr	
(to) say: Say it in English. 1 Ex	Sag(t) es auf Englisch!	stairs 7 A 2	Treppe(nstufen)	
school: at school 1 A 5	in der Schule	stamp 6 A 3	(Brief-)Marke	
sea 4 A 10	Meer	(to) start (sth.) 6 A 2	(mit etwas) anfangen	
season p. 47, 5	Jahreszeit; Saison	(to) stay 7 A 10	bleiben	
second p. 57, 1	Sekunde	stereo 8 T	Stereo, Stereo-	
(to) see 4 A 7	sehen	still 3 A 7	(immer) noch	
See you soon. 5 A 9	Tschüs. Bis bald.	still 6 T	trotzdem, dennoch	
(to) sell 8 A 10	verkaufen	(to) stop 5 Ex	aufhören; (an)halten, stoppen	
sentence 5 Ex	Satz	street: in Sandfield Street 4 A 3	in der Sandfield-Straße	
September p. 47, 1	September	in the street 4 A 3	auf der Straße	
(to) share sth. (with sb.) 7 A 4	(sich) etwas (mit jm.) teilen, etwas gemeinsam benutzen	strong 4 A 10	stark; kräftig	
		summer p. 47, 5	Sommer	
she 1 A 6	sie	sun 3 A 11	Sonne	
shelf; shelves 7 A 2	Bord, (Regal-)Brett; Regal	Sunday 4 A 6	Sonntag	
(to) shine 3 A 11	scheinen	sweets 8 A 4	Süßigkeiten, Bonbons	
shop 3 A 3	Laden, Geschäft	(to) swim 3 A 11	schwimmen	
pet shop 4 A 3	Tierhandlung	swimming-pool 3 A 10	Schwimmbad, Schwimmbecken	
repair shop 3 A 7	Reparaturwerkstatt für Fahrräder			
(shop) assistant 8 A 10	Verkäufer, Verkäuferin	**T**		
short 1 Ex	kurz	table 5 A 7	Tisch	
(to) shut 6 Ww	schließen, zumachen	table-tennis 6 A 3	Tischtennis	
silly 5 Ex	albern, dumm, doof, blöd	(to) take 5 A 3	(mit)nehmen; (hin)bringen, (weg)bringen	
(to) sing 4 A 8	singen	(to) take photos 6 A 3	fotografieren, Fotos/Bilder machen	
singer 5 T	Sänger, Sängerin	(to) take the dog for a walk 4 A 5	mit dem Hund rausgehen	
sir 6 A 10	Anrede, z. B. für den Lehrer/einen Kunden im Laden	(to) talk to sb. 3 A 9	mit jm. sprechen, reden; sich mit jm. unterhalten	
sister 1 A 4	Schwester			

tall 1 A 6	groß *(bei Menschen)*; hoch
tea 6 A 8	Tee
teacher 1 A 1	Lehrer, Lehrerin
(tele)phone: (to) be on the (tele)phone 3 A 9	am Telefon sein, gerade telefonieren
(to) (tele)phone sb. 8 T	jn. anrufen
television 3 A 5	Fernsehen, Fernseher
terrible 2 A 6	schrecklich, furchtbar
Thank you. 2 Ex	Danke (schön).
Thanks. 2 Ex	Danke (schön).
that 5 A 8	der/die/das (da), jener (-e, -es) (dort)
that's ... = that is ... 1 A 4	das ist ...
... that ... 8 T	..., dass ...
the 1 A 6	der, die, das; die *(Plural)*
their 2 A 4	ihr, ihre
them 5 A 9	ihnen, sie
there 5 T	da, dort; dahin, dorthin
there is/are 4 A 3	da ist/sind, es gibt/sind
these 5 A 8	diese, die (hier)
they 1 A 9	sie
thing 4 A 8	Ding, Sache
(to) think 7 A 11	meinen, glauben, denken
I don't think so. 7 T	Das finde/glaube ich nicht.
I think so. 7 T	Ich glaube (ja).
this 5 A 8	dieser (-e, -es), der/die/das (hier)
this is ... 2 A 1	dies/das (hier) ist ...
this morning/ afternoon/ evening 8 T	heute Morgen/ Nachmittag/ Abend
those 5 A 8	die/diese (da), jene (dort)
through 7 T	durch, hindurch
Thursday 4 A 6	Donnerstag
(to) tidy up 7 A 9	aufräumen
tiger 4 A 7	Tiger
till 6 A 1	bis *(Zeitangabe)*
time 3 A 1	Zeit
What time is it? 3 A 1	Wie spät ist es?
tin: a tin of ... 5 A 7	eine Dose ..., eine Büchse ...
tired 3 A 11	müde
to 3 A 10	zu, nach, in
It's ten miles to .... 3 T	Es sind zehn Meilen bis (nach/zu) ....
quarter to ten p. 57, 1	Viertel vor zehn
today p. 47, 4	heute
together 3 A 10	zusammen, miteinander
toilet 4 Ww	Toilette
tomorrow p. 47, 6	morgen
tomorrow morning p. 47, 6	morgen früh

tonight 4 A 2	heute Abend/Nacht	(to) walk 6 A 2	(zu Fuß) gehen, laufen	Why? 5 A 3	Warum? Weshalb?	
..., too. 1 A 6	auch	wall 7 A 2	Wand; Mauer	Why not ...? 5 A 3	Warum nicht ...? Könnten wir nicht ...?	
too small 4 A 2	zu klein	(to) wash 7 A 9	waschen, sich waschen			
(to) touch 4 A 4	berühren, anfassen	(to) wash the dishes 7 A 9	(das Geschirr) spülen, abwaschen	wife 7 T	(Ehe-)Frau	
town Intro	Stadt			window 4 A 3	Fenster, Schaufenster	
train p. 57, 3	(Eisenbahn-)Zug	watch p. 57, 1	(Armband-)Uhr	winter p. 47, 5	Winter	
by train 6 A 2	mit dem Zug	My watch is wrong. 6 Ex	Meine Uhr geht falsch.			
tree 4 A 8	Baum			with 2 A 4	mit	
(to) try 4 Ex	versuchen, probieren	(to) watch sth./sb. 3 A 5	sich etwas ansehen; jm. zuschauen, jn. beobachten	with (the girls) 3 T	bei (den Mädchen)	
Tuesday 4 A 6	Dienstag					
turn: It's your turn. 4 A 6	Du bist an der Reihe.			woman, women 3 A 11	Frau, Frauen	
		(to) watch TV 3 A 5	fernsehen			
TV = television 3 A 5	Fernsehen, Fernseher	way: I'm on my way (to ...). 3 A 10	Ich bin auf dem Weg/ unterwegs (nach ...).	word 1 Ex	Wort	
				work 7 A 5	Arbeit	
(to) watch TV 3 A 5	fernsehen			(to) be at work 7 A 5	am Arbeitsplatz sein, arbeiten	
on TV 5 T	im Fernsehen	we 1 A 10	wir			
		(to) wear 6 A 1	(Kleidung) tragen, anhaben	(to) go to work 7 A 5	zur Arbeit gehen	
U						
		Wednesday 4 A 6	Mittwoch	(to) work 3 A 3	arbeiten	
uncle 5 A 8	Onkel	week 4 A 6	Woche	would like: I'd like ... 8 Ex	Ich hätte/möchte gern ...	
under 7 A 3	unter	50p a week 8 A 3	50 Pence pro Woche			
(to) understand 7 Ww	verstehen, begreifen	weekend: at the weekend 5 A 2	am Wochenende	(to) write p. 47, 4	schreiben	
uniform 6 A 1	Uniform	welcome: You're welcome. 5 T	Bitte (sehr). Nichts zu danken. Gern geschehen.	(to) write to sb. 5 Ex	an jn. schreiben	
unit 1 A 1	Lektion, Lehrbucheinheit					
upstairs 7 A 2	oben (im Haus); nach oben	Well, ... 3 A 2	Nun, ...; Also, ...	wrong 4 T	falsch	
		wet 4 T	nass; feucht	My watch is wrong. 6 Ex	Meine Uhr geht falsch.	
us 5 A 9	uns	What? 1 A 3	Was?			
(to) use 6 A 7	benutzen, gebrauchen, verwenden	What ...? 3 Ww	Was für ein(e) ...?, Welcher/Welche/ Welches ...?	**Y**		
usually 7 A 5	normalerweise, gewöhnlich	What date is it (today)? p. 47, 4	Der Wievielte ist heute?	year p. 47, 1	Jahr	
				yellow 7 A 3	gelb	
		What is it? 8 T	Was ist denn (los)?	yes 1 A 3	ja	
V		What's your name? 1 A 3	Wie ist dein Name? Wie heißt du?	you Intro; 3 A 9	du, Sie, ihr; dir, Ihnen, euch; dich, Sie, euch	
very 1 A 6	sehr	What time is it? 3 A 1	Wie spät ist es?	you 7 A 9	*hier:* man	
village 5 A 4	Dorf			You're welcome. 5 T	Bitte (sehr). Nichts zu danken. Gern geschehen.	
		When? p. 47, 5	Wann?			
W		When's your birthday? 5 A 1	Wann hast du Geburtstag?	young 2 A 6	jung	
		when ... 7 A 10	wenn ...	your 1 A 1	dein(e); Ihr(e); euer, eure	
(to) wait for sb. 3 A 9	auf jn. warten	Where? 1 A 2; 5 A 3	Wo? Wohin?	Yours, ... 5 Ex	dein(e) ...; ihr(e) ...; euer/eure ... *(am Briefende)*	
walk: (to) take the dog for a walk 4 A 5	mit dem Hund rausgehen	Where are you from? 1 A 2	Wo kommst du her?			
		white 2 A 6	weiß	youth club 8 A 7	Jugendklub, Jugendzentrum	
		Who? 2 A 2	Wer?			

Bildquellen: Aerofilms Limited, Boreham Wood (S. 5); British Tourist Authority (S. 100/101); Cornelsen-Velhagen & Klasing, Berlin (S. 45); David Dore, Guildford (S. 58); Michael Ferguson, Berlin (S. 98); Angelika Fischer, Berlin (S. 81); P. de Kleine, Berlin (S. 83, 96); J. Walmsley, Biggleswade (S. 68/69).
Einband: Ingeborg Ullrich, Berlin.

Liedquelle: *My Friend Jack* (S. 39) by Ken Wilson, © 1977 Cornelsen-Velhagen & Klasing, Berlin.